REGULATING
CONFUSION

REGULATING CONFUSION

Samuel Johnson and the Crowd

THOMAS REINERT

Duke University Press   Durham and London   1996

© 1996 Duke University Press

All rights reserved

Printed in the United States of America on acid-free paper ∞

Typeset in Adobe Garamond by Keystone Typesetting, Inc.

Library of Congress Cataloging-in-Publication Data appear on the last printed
page of this book.

Contents

Acknowledgments

Chapter 5 first appeared in a slightly different form in *Studies in English Literature: 1500–1900* (1988) 28.

I would like to thank the following teachers and colleagues for reading early and late versions of this book: Laura Brown, Cynthia Chase, Jonathan Culler, Timothy Peltason, Lawrence Rosenwald, Margery Sabin, and Harry Shaw. I am especially grateful to Neil Hertz for his advice and help. And I would like to thank Nick Halpern, William Flesch, and Laura Quinney, who helped lay down some of this book's basic ideas.

Introduction

Among readers of Samuel Johnson there has been an effort over the last fifty years to personalize his moral thought.[1] Johnson, we are told, was an empiricist;[2] he accumulated observations on human life from experience without regard to prior beliefs or expectations. He espoused a rigorously moral view of human life, but refrained from systematizing his observations. The material pressures, complications, and nuances of the everyday concerned him more than the impersonal grandeur of philosophical abstractions or of political debates.[3] As a moralist, he sought general truth, but as an empiricist he respected the authority of specific facts. For these reasons, he conceived of moral reflection not so much as a matter of maxims and the didactic inculcation of rules, but as a matter of exercising judgment. He told stories in his moral essays designed to illustrate the complexity of real experience and the necessity for careful reflection in particular cases.[4] General adherence to moral rules was not enough.

Behind Johnson's personal style of moral thought, critics have argued, there was a conviction that what was true for individuals must also be true for humanity as a whole.[5] He believed in the uniformity of human nature. The differences between individuals showed the influence of temperament and circumstances, and the differences between cultures showed the variety of expressive forms, but the materials of human nature—passions, reason, needs, judgment—were the same for everyone. But its uniformity did not make human nature codifiable or systematic. It was uniform but nonetheless complex. The best way to comment on it was to examine specific examples: specific lives and circumstances.[6] In his preference for biography and for literary characters who represent whole species, critics have argued, Johnson expressed this basic belief in the continuity between the personal and the universal.

Critics have offered various models to represent this figure of continuity, or this basic aesthetic preference, in Johnson's writing. William Edinger suggests the Hegelian and Eliotic figure of the "concrete universal"; he puts Johnson in a tradition of humanist realism that includes Homer, Richardson, Flaubert, and Joyce.[7] Jean Hagstrum suggests that universality and particularity can simply float loosely but without contradiction in the concept of "nature."[8] W. J. Bate describes Johnson's writing as the product of a kind of distillation and compression: after years of experience, Johnson discerned general outlines of human behavior, general patterns and regularities, but because of the wealth of his experience, his pictures of life, while general, comprise innumerable distinctive details that give them particularity and weight.[9] All of these critics stress that Johnson's style is "living" and "organic," as opposed to mechanical and formulaic.[10]

These critics exemplify some of the predilections of New Criticism as it was practiced in the forties and fifties: in particular, the predilection for "organic" form, and for attention to specific cases and sensuous experience. The organicism and the psychological bent of this writing are at odds with more recent (though no longer new) lines of thought in literary theory, and now no longer seem as inevitable a framework for reading as they did earlier. The interest of reading for the "inorganic" has in the meantime become apparent and widely familiar; and for someone steeped in this newer critical atmosphere, Johnson is appealing less for his realism and humanism than for his impersonality and his rhetorical dissonances.

The present book is about the topic of the crowd, a topic which evokes the disjunction between the general and the particular as a fact of social experience. Johnson raises the topic usually as a reminder of an individual person's insignificance. "[Y]ou are only one atom of the mass of humanity, and have neither such virtue nor vice, as that you should be singled out for supernatural favours or afflictions."[11] "No place affords a more striking conviction of the vanity of human hopes, than a publick library; for who can see the wall crouded on every side by mighty volumes . . . without considering how many hours have been wasted."[12] "It is long before we are convinced of the small proportion which every man bears to the collective body of mankind" (R 146, 5:15). Johnson writes of the world as a place where one is neglected "in the mighty heap of human calamity" (R 99, 4:166), and no amount of wishing or working can assure a person at last a measure of public attention. The crowd in Johnson is not a power one productively engages with, but a power that isolates, obstructs, and humiliates.

Walter Benjamin, in an essay on Baudelaire, suggests that crowds transform and undermine the feeling of collective experience, in particular the experience of the "concrete universal" which critics are apt to ascribe to Johnson. Benjamin finds in urban culture a decline of what he calls "experience in the strict sense."[13] Such experience has this structure of the "concrete universal": in it, "certain contents of the individual past combine with material of the collective past" (159). Benjamin claims that it was an experience produced by "rituals with their ceremonies, [and] their festivals" (159). In urban culture a ritual sense of time, with its wealth of involuntary memory, gives way to empty chronological time, which marks the distinctness of each moment (163). City dwellers instinctively break their impressions into small, discrete units. Newspapers work to "isolate what happens" from the reader by keeping the news fresh, brief, and disconnected (158); and the "smooth functioning of the social mechanism" blunts the feeling of being dependent on others: "The inhabitant of the great urban centers"— Benjamin quotes Paul Valéry—reverts [because of comfort] to a state of savagery—that is, of isolation" (174). Benjamin suggests that disconnection becomes a feature of everyday consciousness: he quotes Baudelaire, who speaks of a man plunging into the crowd as a "*kaleidoscope* equipped with consciousness" (175). Benjamin notes in a passage from Poe that even the individuals in the crowd seem to be breaking into pieces: they have detached-looking ears, bald heads, shifty eyes, and make weird, jerky movements (171). Georg Lukács, writing of Zola's novels, observes a similar disintegration of experience due to the crowd. The characters "act without a pattern, either side by side or else in completely chaotic fashion."[14] They have no sense of the social bonds between them: the "social motives which, unknown even to themselves, govern their actions, thoughts and emotions, grow increasingly shallow" (143). But at the same time disconnected details of local color swarm around them: they "form a gigantic backdrop in front of which tiny, haphazard people move to and fro and live haphazard lives" (92).

These effects of the crowd raise questions about moral reflection, especially of the sort ascribed to Johnson by his readers. Claims about the uniformity of human nature strike an odd note when the author feels every day the distance between himself and the crowds of strangers flowing around him. Confidence that one person's story illuminates those of all people is surprising when the pressure of urban isolation seems to inculcate incessantly a contrary lesson. To the extent that Johnson expresses such a confidence, he invites critical speculation. One wonders about his psychological defenses and his ideological delusions. Style, according to Max Horkheimer and Theodor Adorno, reconciles "the general and particular, . . . the rule and the specific demands of the subject matter";[15] as a reconciler it is "always ideology." For style clashes with and conceals the absence of real, social integration. "The unity of style . . . expresses in each case the different structure of social power, and not the obscure experience of the oppressed in which the general was enclosed" (130). Johnson's humanistic style of moral reflection would seem, in the context of the crowd, to perform such an ideological function. Horkheimer and Adorno add that style is essential to art—it gives expression "that force without which life flows away unheard" (130)—but that artists are not prisoners of style. The greatest of them violate their style's demands, and in doing so, expose the ideological deception which the work threatens to promulgate (131). It is accordingly interesting to notice the slippages in Johnson's style, especially in passages about the crowd.

It is difficult, though, to say what a crowd is and what counts as an ideologically distorted perception of it. This difficulty arises partly as a perceptual limitation. Encountering a crowd is a version of Kant's mathematical sublime: it dramatizes how readily imagination outruns sensory apprehension. Wordsworth's experience of London crowds is a famous example: "How often in the overflowing streets / Have I gone forwards with the crowd, and said / Unto myself, 'The face of everyone / That passes by me is a mystery.' "[16] Wordsworth writes that the oppression of this mystery weighed on him so heavily that his mind began to totter: "the shapes before my eyes became / A second-sight procession . . . / And all the ballast of familiar life—/ The present, and the past, hope, fear, all stays, / All laws of acting, thinking, speaking man—/ Went from me" (258–60; 601–7).

Wordsworth's experience jibes with Elias Canetti's claim that the sense of a distinct personal self disintegrates in a crowd. This is the essential characteristic of crowding, Canetti believes: "As soon as a man has surrendered himself to the crowd, he ceases to fear its touch. Ideally, all are equal there; no distinctions count, not even that of sex. The man pressed against him is the same as himself. He feels as he feels himself. Suddenly it is as though everything were happening in one and the same body."[17] Johnson expresses something of this idea when he says that the crowds at taverns help him forget himself.[18] The crowd is not properly an object of experience; rather, it dissolves self-consciousness. Benjamin suggests that crowds induce shock in those unprepared for them psychologically. People prepare themselves by finding ways, not to help their impressions enter experience, but to prevent them from doing so. The need to ward off shocks is so great that an urban poet like Baudelaire registers the city primarily in the ways he avoids referring to it (167–68).

Much of eighteenth-century London culture, according to Richard Sennett, developed from just such a need to find protection against the shock of the city crowds. The population had grown in the preceding century from 150,000 to 700,000, mostly as a result of the migration of workers from the country; by 1800, the number had risen to 900,000.[19] Changes in neighborhoods made streets less places to meet than to pass through (55); and the expansion of trade encouraged businesses to grow away from family ownership (58). Such changes, Sennett argues, "served to define the stranger as an unknown . . . who could not easily be placed through factual inquiries" (59). London seemed overgrown and overwhelming; it was the "Great Wen," running over with crowds (51–52); and according to Sennett, the elaborate artifice of dress and manners in eighteenth-century London arose as a defense against this threat of being overwhelmed. Headdresses, beauty marks, and costumes were coded tokens by which Londoners disclosed at a glance their class standing, sexual inclination, profession, even political attitude. Their preoccupation with manners, rules of decorum, and codes of public behavior similarly responded, Sennett argues, to their need to clarify and regulate a public world which had grown too confused and multifarious to be grasped by an unprepared imagination.[20]

What about that claim itself? How does a scholar like Sennett or Benjamin discover characteristic responses to being in a crowd? If it is difficult or impossible to apprehend a crowd, it would seem difficult by the same token to say how crowds feel about themselves. Sennett does not try to show that masses of individual Londoners felt panic-stricken because of the city's overcrowding; he nowhere describes them seeking relief, consciously or unconsciously, in the protection of artificial public manners. "London" developed those manners collectively; or rather, the city's demographics were linked to them in a "logical relationship": "[T]he first of the four structures of public life—[its vast, anonymous crowds]—came to have a logical relationship to the second structure—the codes of belief bridging theater and society. The first was a matter of material disorder; the second an emotional order built upon it; the order was a response to the disorder, but also transcendence of it" (64). It is "logical" to deduce that the manners of the time protected Londoners against anxiety and disorientation, but it would be hard to show, or to believe, that particular citizens felt this tension as they put on their wigs and beauty marks. The logic concerns the relationship between mass phenomena, not between particular persons. It does not lend itself to explanation by storytelling. Sennett is not particularly proposing that crowds have a spirit of their own, distinct from the feelings of their individual members, such that they could be placed as actors in their own impersonal drama. Rather, he is just pointing out a logical connection; he argues analytically, not chronologically or narratively. In doing so, he solves the problem of how to represent the feelings of crowds: he abandons the rhetorical framework of personal experience and narration; but he raises the question of whether the analysis then represents something real or just the consequences of talking in a peculiar way. Who was feeling the anxiety and the relief in eighteenth-century London if it was not quite individual persons and not quite the city as such? To the extent that it seems necessary or not to return Sennett's argument to the storytelling mode implied in that question, his argument seems more cogent or less.

Though there are many traces of the crowd's effect on Johnson, it is part of the interest of crowds that they do not simply exist, but have to be imagined. They constitute a massive social fact of life in eighteenth-century London, but they also represent an epistemological block. They are experienced as an occasion to sense the limits of experience, and to reflect upon the extent to which our notions about "massive social facts" are intellectual phantasms. In writing about Johnson on crowds, it is valuable to try to understand the social circumstances of his work; but at the same time, the topic keeps raising the thought that, in writing at least, social circumstances are also dreamt up by writers.

———

The title of this book comes from a passage in the "Preface" to the *Dictionary* which describes Johnson's encounter with a crowd not of people but of words. The passage illustrates his style of moral reflection in the midst of the crowd:

> When I took the first survey of my undertaking [to write the *Dictionary*], I found our speech copious without order, and

energetick without rules: wherever I turned my view, there was perplexity to be disentangled, and confusion to be regulated; choice was to be made out of boundless variety, without any established principle of selection; adulterations were to be detected, without a settled test of purity; and modes of expression to be rejected or received, without the suffrages of any writers of classical reputation or acknowledged authority.[21]

Faced with "boundless variety," he wants to "regulate confusion." He does it in more distinctly moral contexts, but even here his concern is not just lexicographical but moral, as one gathers from the oddly emphatic use of the first person, and from the morally tainted specter of linguistic fertility run amok. This is more pronounced in the foregoing paragraph, which imagines English as an infested garden: it has been "suffered to spread, under the direction of chance, into wild exuberance; resigned to the tyranny of time and fashion; and exposed to the corruptions of ignorance, and caprices of innovation" (234). Into this scene of chance, wild exuberance, and corruption, Johnson comes as a legislator, an outside observer who takes a "survey" of the chaos and undertakes to regulate it.[22]

The language is confused because it is vast and multifarious. In this passage Johnson speaks of its "boundless variety"; later he refers to the "boundless chaos of a living speech" (241). He cannot collect all the senses of many words, so great "is the exuberance of signification" which they have obtained (247). The addition of particles to verbs produces "innumerable expressions . . . , of which some appear wildly irregular, being so far distant from the sense of the simple words, that no sagacity will be able to trace the steps by which they arrived at the present use" (244). The language is "variable by the caprice of every one that speaks it"; and so some words are "hourly shifting their relations" (245). Their meaning is so "loose and general" that it is "hard to trace them through the maze of variation, to catch them on the brink of utter inanity, to circumscribe them by any limitations, or interpret them by any words of distinct and settled meaning" (245).

The vastness of the numbers of people speaking the language helps breed this confusion. It allows mistakes and gratuitous distortions to become a part of the language. Johnson speaks, for instance, of "illiterate writers" who, "by publick infatuation," gain a large audience and propagate mistakes. It is easy to deplore the carelessness and the gratuitousness of such effects; the misspelling of certain words can make even the most anti-authoritarian English professor feel that civilization is collapsing. But after errors attain some degree of currency, perspective shifts, and one regards them as intrinsic features of the language. Verb-and-particle combinations, for example, which defy attempts to derive their meaning from the individual words, may likely have grown up through the cumulative effect of generations of misspeaking. Johnson writes of spelling "defects" which "are not errours in orthography, but spots of barbarity impressed so deep in the *English* language, that criticism can never wash them away" (236). He goes on to discriminate them from "vulgar" errors and accidents; but he has to import a nonlinguistic set of distinctions (class distinctions) to sort out what appears, linguistically, to be a distinction without a difference.

If language regularly accommodates and naturalizes errors, this is because usage does not derive from a fixed code of rules and an immutable set of principles. It is subject to change because it follows the authority, not of principle, but of "general agreement."

> *Swift,* in his petty treatise on the *English* language, allows that new words must sometimes be introduced, but proposes that none should be suffered to become obsolete. But what makes a word obsolete, more than general agreement to forbear it? and how shall it be continued, when it conveys an offensive idea, or recalled into the mouths of mankind, when it has once become unfamiliar by disuse, and unpleasing by unfamiliarity? (257)

An agreement determines usage, but the agreement is made in the moment of usage itself. Its authority, in this view, is not separate from actual practice, and does not provide a more stable ground for it. The fact of it is usage's only authority; language is to be spoken a certain way because it happens to be spoken that way. But this view cannot distinguish, on principle, between linguistic order and accidents. There is simply the decree of "general agreement," which is indeterminately authoritative and arbitrary.

The power of this decree blocks the reformer's search for a definable and decisive ground from which to resolve conflicts in the language. Though it is possible to locate sources of linguistic change, they are not sources of authority. Johnson speaks of large social shifts that transform a language—migrations, invasions, commerce, the rise of a leisure class—but they give way to one another over time because language acknowledges no power absolutely. As usage mutates through generations of social change, it demonstrates that language fundamentally lacks propriety. Language does not have an ideal form. In this sense, it is merely given. It is a bare fact, not so much because we know what it is by experience, as because we cannot say what it ought to be.

Given this conception of language as a "boundless" protean activity, a crowd phenomenon without limits or formal propriety, Johnson is hard pressed not merely to regulate its confusion, but to say what "regulation" would mean. But at the end of the "Preface" he describes the effect he thinks the *Dictionary* might have, despite the intractableness and elusiveness of the problems posed by the language:

> If the changes that we fear be thus irresistible, what remains but to acquiesce with silence, as in other insurmountable distresses of humanity? It remains that we retard what we cannot repel, that we palliate what we cannot cure. Life may be lengthened by care, though death cannot be ultimately defeated: tongues, like governments, have a natural tendency to degeneration; we have long preserved our constitution, let us make some struggles for our language. (258)

This formulation ascribes two kinds of authority to Johnson, one practical, the other moral and symbolic. The *Dictionary's* practical effect, he hopes, will be to slow down the language's change. This is a compromise between the reformer's desire to preserve the language intact forever and the irresistible forces of change ranged against him.

But it is not enough to say that Johnson wants to slow down changes in the language. He has a tragic weightiness in the passage that comes from his metaphorical assumption that language has a life and must inevitably die. He is struggling not just against linguistic change, but against decay and death. The metaphor personalizes the language. It gives it the shapeliness that Johnson has been saying it lacks. It attributes to it a direction. In doing so, though it does not establish an ideal linguistic form or a standard of purity—to do that, it would have to freeze the language or "embalm" it, in Johnson's phrase, and a "living" speech, he implies, is bound to keep changing—it nevertheless raises, like a ghost, a feeling of urgency, a cloud of pathos. When a language is in danger of dying, the lexicographer who forestalls its decline obeys something akin to a moral obligation. He struggles with a general paradox of living: one wants to preserve life, but since mutability is one of life's essential characteristics, the attempt to preserve it has to be full of resignation while also remaining passionate.

This dilemma keeps the ideal of a pure form fluttering on the horizon: it makes sense to favor life and to shun forces of decay—such contrasts form a comprehensible moral standard—but only because it is impossible to preserve life absolutely. By construing language as "living speech," Johnson summons up this kind of ghostly, inaccessible, but nevertheless (for the lexicographer) passionately interesting shadow of an ideal form. Though he does not establish a fixed standard, he instills in his project a sense of purposefulness, no less earnest for being vaguely or metaphorically defined. He will not be able to say definitively that certain usages are right or wrong, but he will feel that it is urgently important to try to say so and that in some loose, sloppy way he can, the way characters in Defoe can try to live so as to ward off the plague though they have no idea what causes it. They take symbolic rituals of prevention very seriously.[23]

In other words, "regulating" confusion means construing the language figuratively as a living entity; superimposing on it—on its boundless scattering—the metaphor of organic integration.[24] The appeal to "living speech" does not feel isolated or whimsical. It comes at a difficult moment in the essay where Johnson is trying to define what kind of authority he has in the absence of any absolute standards; and also it jibes with the "Preface"'s surprisingly mournful, personalizing account of lexicography as a moral struggle marked by noble diligence and laden with pathos. By contrast to more modern dictionaries, which determinedly obscure the identities of their contributors, Johnson poignantly dramatizes his weary labors. The idea that a single man wrote the *Dictionary* seems essential to the whole project. Everyone who holds the book's massive volumes feels the marvel of that idea. The *Dictionary* vehemently asserts the individual's power to order "boundless chaos," and offers its own design as an exemplary pattern. One sign of the peculiar kind of seriousness—the moral seriousness—Johnson ascribes to the singleness of his authorship is that he declares several times (252, 254, 259) that the task was in fact too big for him; yet it seems to have been inconceivable to him that he might have formed a committee and parceled the work out. Some errors, he apologizes, were inevitable in so vast a work: "a whole life cannot be spent upon syntax and etymology, and . . . even a whole life would not be sufficient" (259).

The tone of this admission is characteristic. Johnson wants to make the point that he did his best, but he gives the idea so much weight that it overwhelms the mundane practical view of his problem. His perspective is affectingly moral and personal. Instead of conveying correct information by whatever effective means possible, the *Dictionary*'s task seems to be to illustrate how hard Johnson worked and how weak a creature man is. The obvious solution of forming a committee is beside the point once the project is understood in these terms. According to a well-known story in Boswell's *Life*, Johnson computed how many Frenchmen he was worth given that it took forty members of the French Academy forty years to perform what he planned to do in three (1:186). The "Preface" disapproves of academies in general on the grounds that they "multiply dependency." What is striking about this is not so much the boastfulness but the belligerent assertion of the individual's relevance or viability in a circumstance where its viability is so manifestly questionable. It seems reasonable to see this fervor in his metaphor of "living speech" as well.

Johnson stresses, too, that specific decisions about usage devolved upon his personal acumen and sensibility. Sometimes he derived spellings etymologically, sometimes on the basis of custom (237); sometimes he admitted obsolete words because he found them in favorite authors, sometimes only because he liked them (243); sometimes he gave the literal meaning of words which he was unsure had ever been used in any but a metaphorical sense (247). Since "choice was to be made out of boundless variety, without any established principle of selection," he evidently chose according to a hodgepodge of considerations, some linguistic, some not; and what held them together and gave them coherence was the coherence of his personal discrimination, some intuitive sense he had of rightness, the acuity of his ear.

Johnson is ambivalent about this personalizing tendency. The sense of language's impersonality is persistent, as in the opposition between a "whole life" and "etymology and syntax." He thinks that the language is alive, but his belief that it is decaying indicates how fragile its life is in his imagining of it. Its life seems an anomaly, stolen from the midst of disorder. He is diffident about his own assumption of authority as well. He adopts a pathos-laden, moral tone when he describes his hardships; but he also tries to strip himself of personal importance. In his icy philosophic farewell he claims that his personal life has become a dreary solitude in which he merely waits for death, and in his introduction he presents himself as a hapless drudge. The passage about regulating confusion enumerates his impossible tasks with a certain luxuriousness. He multiplies eagerly the ways in which he lacks authority. He speaks of his undertaking as one of the "lower employments of life" and the lexicographer as one of those "unhappy mortals . . . whom mankind have considered, not as the pupil, but the slave of science, the pionier of literature, doomed only to remove rubbish and clear obstructions from the paths" (234).

One takes this as a moral meditation on resignation, but also as a luscious exercise in comic melancholy in which Johnson savors the contours of his abysmal insignificance.[25] He is a "slave," humiliated and kicked aside indifferently by the masters he serves; the passage's sense of humor makes him like one of Beckett's tramps, who become funnier the more abused they are. When he explains that he had had to choose without any principle of selection, detect adulterations without a standard of purity, receive and reject expressions without the help of authorities, he casts himself as a victim of the absurd, like Sisyphus piling rocks or Xerxes lashing the waves. At the same time, it is true, he imagines himself as a legislator; the garden metaphors and the remark about surveying the language for the first time even hint that he is a kind of Adam. He is a reformer and regulator, a sovereign authority; he proposes to establish correct usage, encourage certain words, and proscribe others. But later he sees himself in the passive, glamorless role of a registrar: "[I] do not form, but register the language; [I] do not teach men how they should think, but relate how they have hitherto expressed their thoughts" (253). Personal authority is essential to Johnson's notion of regulating confusion, but it is also hapless and marginal. It provides an array of metaphors for interpreting impersonal processes, but as a metaphor it feels insecure, though necessary.

Johnson writes about different crowds: words, people, desires. He treats them all similarly. The "Preface" suggests why. The crowd is not experiential for him in the sense that he can encounter it, but in the sense that it balks him, it puts his powers in question, makes him doubt the pertinence of his will, or of anyone's will. It devalues the personal. His writing about crowds is consequently about the limits of experience and will, about the relation between the ego and the imagination, and about moral actions which may or may not be ineffectual, strung out as they are between empty talk and hard-headed empiricism.

———

This book addresses itself not only to eighteenth-century scholars but also to contemporary theorists. It is a response to the ambivalence I think many critics must feel about writing literary commentary when it seems important to be concerned with politics. Current literary critics have a strong political conscience; they obey it as a matter of moral principle. Their writing has illustrated literature's myriad political effects. One reason this writing is popular, though, I would guess, is that it struggles against a persistent suspicion—a suspicion that arises easily when one is alone, writing, and thinking about what sort of audience one's writing might find—that one's own work is apt to prove politically negligible. The market for literary criticism is tiny; the influence of literary criticism on political organizations is obscure. The institution of literary studies in the university no doubt leaves a mark on the society's cultural consciousness, but almost certainly not as vivid a mark as those made by dozens of other cultural institutions. As for individual works, few of them have any discernible political effect.

Since it is hard to imagine what assurance would shield critics from suspecting that their work will turn out politically negligible, it is interesting to say what that suspicion feels like, and what it would mean to manage it well. That is what I am supposing Johnson's interest to be. He elaborates on the predicament of someone who feels the burden of public responsibility without knowing how to shoulder it, or even what doing so would look like. His appeal lies in the poise he sustains in the midst of his perplexity.

Currently the problem of literary criticism's political status is particularly related to the theme of the crowd because of the spread of multiculturalism. A politically conscious literary critic is encouraged not only to respect deep differences between cultural traditions and perspectives, but to feel how many perspectives there are, starting with everyday life in the United States, and how rapidly they take turns demanding consideration. Stanley Fish explains that the new historicism aims to accommodate the multifariousness of multicultural politics by cultivating a free-floating, open-ended notion of self, a self responsive to many perspectives because it cannot inhabit any particular one exclusively.[26] The self is "now thought to be not stable but 'multiple, contradictory and in process'" (310). According to the new historicists, we should "reject the exclusionary discourses that presently delimit our perceptions and abrogate our freedom of action in favor of the more flexible and multi-directional mode of being that seems called for by everything we have recently learned about the historicity of our situatedness; we should classify less, remember more, refuse less, and be forever open in a manner befitting a creature always in process" (310).

Fish argues strenuously against the new historicist aim: "The trouble with this advice is that it is impossible to follow" (310). One cannot determine to be open in general, but only with respect to specific things, like student comments or the consideration of sex and race as criteria in school admissions. "But of course *that* kind of openness is nothing more (or less) than a resolution to be differently closed, to rearrange the categories and distinctions within which some actions seem to be desirable and others less so" (310). No other kind of openness is available to us. We cannot live according to what Catherine Gallagher calls "indeterminate negativity," because, as Fish puts it, "it demands from a wholly situated creature a mode of action or thought (or writing) that is free from the entanglements of situations and the lines of demarcation they declare" (311). The irony of the new historicist political aspiration, according to Fish, is that it asks us to be ahistorical (311).

Fish does not see any reason to be discontent with our "situatedness" ("try it, you'll like it," he says pleasantly [315]). But might one not still feel, following his train of thought, that the hugeness and the multifariousness of general political life threatened to overwhelm the particular web of concerns one person was able to be "open" to? Not every important political matter crystallizes into a scene in which particular actors can resolve to be open in some ways and closed in others. Political questions have an impersonal as well as a personal dimension. When Fish describes the logical constraints on the notion of a situated self, he obeys a pragmatist's instinct for concentrating on the possible. But the new historicist conception of a "multiple, contradictory" self living out its "indeterminate negativity" indulges the imaginative extravagance that beckons when it appears that what is personally possible does not exhaust the field of the politically important.

For a critic who acknowledges Fish's reasonableness but who shares the new historicist's respect for the impersonal, "situatedness" is bound to provoke the discontent that Fish repudiates. Political earnestness struggles with a feeling of ineffectuality; a sense of theatrical self-aggrandizement mingles with questions of moral principle. It feels complacent to recommend, as Fish does, that we concern ourselves simply with what we are really capable of doing; and it seems quixotic to try to match the multifariousness of the political with some expanded, multiple version of the self.

The present work does not try to resolve this dilemma. It is a response to the possibility that the dilemma is unresolvable. It turns to Johnson because of the example of intelligence and discrimination he offers as he faces a roughly similar problem. He has Fish's sense of the necessary particularity of experience and of judgments on experience; but he shares the view of eighteenth-century social theorists that the movement of large masses and institutions follows a logic distinct from that of personal relationships, and that in various ways it overpowers and neutralizes them. Like Fish, he feels the impossibility of staying open to all perspectives; but because crowds affect him as great and powerful, it seems to him a grave matter that we cannot understand them, and his concern casts a shadow over all of his writing. He writes about what it is like to be preoccupied with personal interests when a consciousness of the public world makes them seem trivial.

What he writes is probably more valuable as spectacle than as advice. Since there is only a rough analogy here between his predicament and our own, there can be little question of looking to him for explanations or solutions. But in perplexity, we do not always look for solutions. Sometimes we only look for perspicuous statements of comparable perplexities.

One

The Desire for Fame

According to sentimentalist social theory in the eighteenth century, moral action finds its natural home in small societies.[1] Benevolence, the source of moral action, is natural to humans, and it expresses itself, in the Earl of Shaftesbury's phrase, as a "herding impulse." As long as this impulse gives rise to a small community, Shaftesbury writes, it guides the spirit of the group: "In less parties, men may be intimately conversant and acquainted with one another. They can there better taste society, and enjoy the common good and interest of a more contracted public. They view the whole compass and extent of their community, and see and know particularly whom they serve, and to what end they associate and conspire."[2] Adam Ferguson, similarly, argues that the moral instincts of mankind appear where we feel ourselves part of a close-knit, well-defined social order: "When we are involved in any of the divisions into which mankind are separated under the denominations of a country, a tribe, or an order of men any way affected by common interests, and guided by communicating passions, the mind recognizes its natural station; the sentiments of the breast, and the talents of the understanding, find their natural exercise."[3]

But mankind's intrinsic sociability, and with it the moral instinct, become obstructed in large societies because they have too much material to contend with. Shaftesbury and Ferguson speak of a breakdown of vision when "society grows vast and bulky" (Shaftesbury 76): no "visible band is formed, no strict alliance" in the "body politic at large" (76); "members can no longer apprehend the common ties of society, nor be engaged by affection in the cause of their country" (Ferguson 363). Shaftesbury observes that sentiment accordingly flags; people cannot feel a strong social impulse toward a group whose outline and identity they cannot readily see: the "close sympathy and conspiring virtue is apt to lose itself, for want of direction, in so wide a field" (75).

Bernard Mandeville, who argues rather for an instinctive selfishness in human nature, nevertheless agrees that moral law might govern the social order in small communities; but it will prohibit the growth of the community beyond certain narrow bounds. Scale proceeds from luxury, self-indulgence, fraud, and other vices, according to Mandeville. If "Mankind could be cured of [these] Failings"—which "they are Naturally guilty of"—they would "cease to be capable of being rais'd into such vast, potent and polite Societies, as they have been."[4]

The sentimentalists argue that the expansion of society has an ambivalent moral consequence. On the one hand, people in a large society are driven by their sociable, sympathizing instinct to form smaller societies within the larger one. "To *cantonise* is natural," writes Shaftesbury, "when the society grows vast and bulky" (76). People long to feel the "confederating charm"; where they cannot feel it naturally, they find ways to produce the feeling artificially: "Distinctions of many kinds are invented. Religious societies are formed. Orders are erected, and their interests espoused and served with the utmost zeal and passion" (76). Within the confines of such social orders, people feel themselves in the "natural station" Ferguson speaks of. "Wisdom, vigilance, fidelity, and fortitude, are the characters requisite in such a scene, and the qualities which it tends to improve" (362). But in the society at large, or in the field of humanity generally, these distinctions breed conflict. They are responsible for political factions, tribal prejudices, and wars between countries. "'[T]is in war that the knot of fellowship is closest drawn," writes Shaftesbury (76). "In territories of considerable extent . . . the national union, in rude ages, is extremely imperfect. Every district forms a separate party; . . . their feuds and animosities give more frequently the appearance of so many nations at war, than of a people united by connections of policy" (Ferguson 364). David Hume observes that the very impulse to be sociable tends to throw people back upon their private interests in a large society, and a general selfishness takes over: since things which are contiguous to them impress them most strongly, they neglect their political interests in an extended society, and concern themselves exclusively with their private circle of friends and business associates.[5]

This line of thought, by linking moral sentiment to a particular social circumstance—that is, the limited circle of personal affection and acquaintance—tends to drain that sentiment of its authority as an ordering principle. Its value comes to seem equivocal. Mandeville explains this consequence in a notoriously robust form. For him, the two spheres of experience here—the private and the public—exist in sharp contrast, and as such they force us to doubt the general application of moral precepts. Vice produces personal misery; but since it is essential to the growth of society as a whole, its wickedness is only relative to one's perspective. One is bound to hate vice, especially if one is victimized by it, but Mandeville urges that one might learn, at any rate, "more patiently to submit to those Inconveniencies, which no Government upon Earth can remedy" (55) as long as one considers the benefits that vice brings to society at large: that is, one should suppress moral judgments in favor of social and economic aims. Mandeville compares this conflict of perspectives to the experience of walking in the London streets: people wish the streets were cleaner "whilst they regard nothing but their own Cloaths and private Conveniency; but when once they consider, that what offends them is the result of the Plenty, great Traffick and Opulency of that mighty City, if they have any Concern in its Welfare, they will hardly ever wish to see the Streets of it less dirty" (57). This contrast of perspectives does not absolutely dispel the authority of moral concerns; but it means that moral philosophy cannot hope to generalize its maxims.

Intellectual historians find in sentimentalist social theory as well

a drift toward an institutionally and economically defined conception of social order, and away from one based on moral precepts.[6]
Though eighteenth-century social philosophers reject Mandeville's
idea that social prosperity requires and depends upon private vice,
they nevertheless tend to affirm his view that, in the analysis of large
masses of people, it is relevant only in a roundabout way, if at all, to
invoke the precepts of traditional moral wisdom. Ferguson claims,
in a Mandevillean moment, that the internal feuds of a nation are
beneficial because the participants "acquire a spirit . . . in their
private divisions, and in the midst of a disorder, otherwise hurtful,
of which the force, on many occasions, redounds to the power of the
state" (364). More generally, society runs on the united strength of
a vast array of businesses and institutions which work out their
proper relations among themselves without the guidance of any
governing intelligence. Society grows by the subdivision of the social work among more and more citizens who know less and less
about the system's total organization. "Nations of tradesmen come
to consist of members, who, beyond their own particular trade, are
ignorant of all human affairs, and who may contribute to the preser-
vation and enlargement of their commonwealth, without making
its interest an object of their regard or attention" (296–97).

To characterize the integration of such isolated figures, who may
or may not be morally upright, Ferguson makes use of the amoral
metaphor of the machine. Speaking of government officials, he
writes that they "are made, like the parts of an engine, to concur to a
purpose, without any concert of their own; and equally blind with
the trader to any general combination, they unite with him, in
furnishing to the state its resources, its conduct, and its force" (297–
98). John Barrell speculates that the image of the machine derives
from efforts, like Pope's *Essay on Man,* to imagine man as a moving
part of a universal machine, his function being "perhaps to 'touch
some wheel' which is invisible to him";[7] but, he says, the idea of the
machine came to have an explanatory power in its own right, and
figures as a metaphor for society not only in Mandeville, but also in
Shaftesbury and Hume (30–31). According to Adam Smith, the
social order in civilized and commercial states is at bottom this one

of a blind integration of human parts. It derives advantages from an educated populace—they are less prone to enthusiasm and superstition, and they are more decent and orderly, and easier to govern, than an ignorant and stupid public. But the division of labor, which lies at the basis of commercial expansion, inevitably narrows the average worker's understanding to a very small circuit of experience. When a man spends his whole life performing a few simple operations, he loses the habit of thought. "Of the great and extensive interests of his country he is altogether incapable of judging."[8] In "barbarous societies, as they are commonly called," every man takes part in all aspects of the social process, and so every man "is in some measure a statesman, and can form a tolerable judgment concerning the interest of the society" (2:303); but a large commercial society, though it would benefit from this kind of well-roundedness among its citizens, not only does not depend on it but operates on a principle antithetical to it.

The sentimentalists insist, against Mandeville, that social order and private virtue can be integrated; still, they write as social historians and theorists, not as purveyors of moral maxims. The impulse to moralize appears in them as a kind of political nostalgia: Ferguson and Smith harken back to the age of barbarous societies where every man was a statesman; Hume invokes the figure of the benevolent magistrate as an anchor of social order (537); and Shaftesbury depicts the calming influence of a moral, enlightened elite laughing to scorn the delusions of public enthusiasm. None of them, though, shows, or particularly cares to show, how the general precepts of traditional moral wisdom hold up, what kind of authority they have, when set against the backdrop of an extensive theoretical distinction between private life and society as a whole.

It is Dr. Johnson's distinction that he does struggle with this problem, following it through a long path of complications, paradoxical conclusions, and doubts about the value of his work. He writes as a determined moralist; but he takes seriously the possibility that the rationale of society at large, the movement of crowds, and the work of institutions in some sense render moral reflections trivial and irrelevant. A whole style of pathos, irony, and black humor grows up around his attempts to get clear in what sense particularly this might or might not be true.[9]

It is to be noted, first, that, for a variety of reasons, including his skepticism about the theory of human nature's innate benevolence, and his hatred of atheism, Johnson did not like any of the social theorists.[10] Mandeville seems to have impressed him the most; Johnson said he "opened my views into real life very much" (*Life* 3:293). According to Mrs. Piozzi, he "took care always loudly to condemn The Fable of the Bees, but not without adding, 'that it was the work of a *thinking man*.'"[11] In conversation he was quite certain that Mandeville was wrong to disjoin social order from personal virtue: "It may happen that good is produced by vice; but not as vice. . . . No, it is clear that the happiness of society depends on virtue" (*Life* 3:293). But in his writing, the figure of the crowd often appears as an agent of moral disorientation, much as it does in the work of the social theorists. It is not a strictly vicious force; but it calls to mind, as London streets do in Mandeville, a perspective from which moral considerations are not relevant.[12]

Johnson rarely takes the crowd as a conscious object of study.[13] It figures into his writing usually metaphorically; it comes in short bursts of reflection that give odd colorings to his tone. Perhaps the most sociological of his essays is *Rambler* No. 99, an essay about benevolence and friendship in which he enters a popular contemporary debate about the Christian injunction to love all mankind equally, but in which he formulates a Shaftesburian theory of crowd behavior. Like Shaftesbury and Hume (and like Feguson, who wrote after him), Johnson believes that benevolence cannot take the totality of mankind as its object, a notion he renders as the impossibility of empathizing with the crowds of big cities: if "man were to feel no incentives to kindness, more than his general tendency to congenial nature, Babylon or London, with all their multitudes, would have to him the desolation of a wilderness; his affections, not compressed into a narrower compass, would vanish like elemental fire, in boundless evaporation" (4:166). Johnson claims that the moral impulses of man in this condition, having too wide a field to work on, would degenerate: "he would abandon himself to the fluctuations of chance without expecting help against any calamity, or feeling any wish for the happiness of others" (4:166). Moral action requires a narrower compass, a more personal setting, than the totality of mankind, or even the multitudes of Babylon and London: Johnson thinks that people fabricate the setting they need, by way of avoiding the dissipation and misery that would come from general benevolence operating alone. Man improves the "condition of his existence, by *superadding* friendship to humanity, and the love of individuals to that of the species" (4:165; my emphasis). And again: because general benevolence, operating alone, would result in misery, the "great community of mankind is therefore necessarily broken into smaller independent societies; these form distinct interests . . . [which] are again separated into subordinate classes and combinations, and social life is perpetually branched out into minuter subdivisions, till it terminates in the last ramifications of private friendship" (4:166–67).

Johnson echoes the sentimentalist theory of "cantonisation" in striking detail here; and he deviates from it just as strikingly. He gives the crowd an even more autonomous power and logic than Shaftesbury does. For Shaftesbury, people form political combinations and factions because their powers of sympathy are overextended in the crowd of society; the fact of crowding balks the herding impulse, but that impulse remains the fundamental driving force behind all social formations, public or private. According to Johnson, the fundamental force is rather crowding and the structural necessity it presents of breaking into small groups.[14] Even friendships are driven by the need to ward off the dissipating effects of crowding. But this means that society is not constructed out of friendships; they are not its building blocks. Though Johnson posits an original "general benevolence," he thinks that the impulse to friendship arises not as a way to refocus that benevolence, as in Shaftesbury, but as a new principle "superadded" to protect the self from "evaporation." Personal affection, on this view, is a secondary psychological phenomenon, a kind of defensive artifice. The deep structure—it is not clear that one actually has an experience of this except as a structural necessity—is the pressure exerted by the undifferentiated crowd.

This is perhaps Johnson's most explicit statement of the idea that the crowd dislocates human relationships; but in metaphorical asides he elaborates on the idea throughout his moral essays. He does not appear to be making a hasty or chance remark here. The crowd has in his writing an autonomous logic; it calls up a distinct style of commentary. On the other hand, again, it does not crystallize as a conscious object of study. Its appeal is that it appears mainly as a warp in his efforts to moralize.

One of the resulting rhetorical features of Johnson's writing is an extreme simplification in the depiction of character. In crowd portraits, people reduce to single identifying traits, such as an occupation or a ruling passion. A writer addressing the public has to contend, for example, with the "man whose sole wish is to accumulate money," with "sportsmen and the men of dress," with "the naturalist" and "the philologer" (R 118, 4:268, 269).[15] This is partly because Johnson views the people in crowds as being driven essentially by self-interest; immediately pressing obligations take up their attention so completely as to define their character. He disencumbers them of all the freight of imagination that torments the figures drawn in his individual portraits. Crowds have no imagination; they do not harass themselves with speculations about the distant future, or indulge themselves with memories of the distant past. "Among the lower classes of mankind," at least as they appear to the aspiring candidate for fame, who thus sees them as a crowd, "there will be found very little desire of any other knowledge, than what may contribute immediately to the relief of some pressing uneasiness"; "nor will the trader or manufacturer easily be persuaded, that much pleasure can arise from the mere knowledge of actions performed in remote regions, or in distant times" (4:267–68). Crowds do not particularly care for fantasy: "The truth is, that very few [people] have leisure from indispensable business, to employ their thoughts upon narrative or characters" (4:268). Crowds take a passionate interest in matters of public dispute, but primarily in those which affect them directly. The public's mind is restricted, for Johnson as for Hume, to the present and immediate. Their interest is fixed, for instance, by adherence to a party: "It is scarcely to be imagined, through how many subordinations of interest, the ardour of party is diffused; and what multitudes fancy themselves affected by every satire" (R 106, 4:202). Such enthusiasms arise out of the narrowness of the public mind: "An object, however small in itself, if placed near to the eye, will engross all the rays of light"; and so it is with "trivial" transactions—disputes between factions: they "swell . . . into importance, when [they] press . . . immediately on our attention" (4:202). Once they are removed to a distance, the crowd loses interest (R 146, 5:16).

Related to the simplification of character is a certain probabilistic language that Johnson uses to describe crowds. In the "Preface to Shakespeare" this is particularly clear. Johnson explains here that individual opinion lacks the critical authority that crowds have by virtue of their impersonality. Successive generations are free from the prejudices and blindnesses which disable the judgment of individual people. An author derives advantages from "personal allusions, local customs, [and] temporary opinions," from "favour and competition," from the vanity he indulges and the indignation he gratifies: all of these are merely personal biases which drop away with time.[16] An author whose work can hold the public's interest without the help of such advantages can be considered to have written in accordance with general truths of human nature. Few "maxims are widely received or long retained but for some conformity with truth and nature" (R 2, 3:11); and the reverse is also true: the test of conformity with truth and nature is that of being so received and retained. This is not necessary for works whose "excellence is . . . absolute and definite" and whose principles are "demonstrative and scientifick" (7:59). But to works "appealing wholly to observation and experience, no other test [of value] can be applied than length of duration and continuance of esteem" (7:59–60).

Johnson ascribes the critical authority of successive generations to the work of comparison which they accomplish. "What mankind have long possessed they have often examined and compared, and if they persist to value the possession, it is because frequent comparisons have confirmed opinion in its favour" (7:60). All criticism is dependent on context and perspective. Judgments about whether a river is deep or a house is lofty, for example, require knowledge of more than the object immediately at hand. Personal opinion is intrinsically narrow because it can rely only on a limited perspective. Multiple generations are more authoritative because they approximate an absolute standard, that is, an absolute context.

Yet this does not mean that personal judgments are necessarily wrong; we approach a true judgment by observing their accumulation, as in the case of Homer: "the poems of Homer we yet know not to transcend the common limits of human intelligence, but by remarking, that nation after nation, and century after century, has been able to do little more than transpose his incidents, new name his characters, and paraphrase his sentiments" (7:60). And conversely, after all these comparisons, it is still possible that our judgment is wrong: "human judgment, though it be gradually gaining upon certainty, never becomes infallible; and approbation, though long continued, may yet be only the approbation of prejudice or fashion" (7:61). The value of successive generations of comparison, then, is not so much that they are necessary to correct judgment or that they prove its correctness; but that they greatly improve the probability that judgment is correct. This is one of the ways in which crowds establish a perspective distinct from that of personal experience: they offer a way of lending authority to opinion by formulating it according to a calculus of probabilities.[17]

Personal experience lacks authority, on this view, not just because it is limited and biased, but because it is in fact experiential. Experience as such has no authority; authority belongs to probability. This is why a crowd has more authority than an individual. Aside from having probability on its side, it allows for probabilistic calculation in the first place, allows for a shift into that logic. In *Rambler* No. 2, for example, Johnson argues that the candidate for fame should have a probabilistic relation to his own value: "It may not be unfit for him who makes a new entrance into the lettered world, so far to suspect his own powers as to believe that he possibly may deserve neglect" (3:13). To determine his chances, he needs to observe the crowd: "For this suspicion, every catalogue of a library will furnish sufficient reason; as he will find it crouded with names of men, who, though now forgotten, were once no less enterprising or confident than himself" (3:13). The perspective of the crowd helps the author see past the contingent veil of his self-love, which may blind him to his real faults; but all the same, it is not a perspective that allows him to "experience" himself. The crowd's authority pushes experience aside to make room for a process of rational guessing.

One way to feel that the crowd has a logic distinct from that of personal experience is to try to become famous. Johnson writes about this attempt often, always in order to inculcate the perception that, in a crowd, the personal counts for nothing. The dispiriting figure of the library catalog appears twice, not only in *Rambler* No. 2, but also in No. 106. In No. 16 a fictional correspondent writes that fame has turned him into a commodity. No. 118 ridicules Cicero's argument that fame is worthless because it cannot spread throughout the world or last through eternity. "A little consideration will indeed teach us, that fame has other limits than mountains or oceans" (3:267). It is limited by the crowd's peculiar movement and style of attention, which make a mockery of Cicero's language of tragic disappointment. In a crowd, a person is simply not very important; disappointment there lacks tragic grandeur. Johnson tells a story in *Rambler* No. 146 of a would-be celebrity who publishes a pamphlet and prepares bravely for a critical response. He is a model of rational restraint. He eschews vanity; he is determined "not to suffer his quiet to be injured by a sensibility too exquisite of praise or blame"; he will "laugh with equal contempt at vain objections and injudicious commendations" (5:13). He asks only to be treated with proper, humane moderation. Morally prepared in this way, he goes out to hear what people have to say; and no one is talking about the pamphlet one way or the other. It is virtuous of him to try to moderate his expectations, but in a crowd, even moderation expects too much. There it is a form of vanity to imagine that vanity counts for anything. Johnson stresses the comic casualness with which the crowd neglects the pamphleteer: violently impatient to hear some word about his work, the man "ranges over the town with restless curiosity, and hears in one quarter of a cricket-match, in another of a pick-pocket; is told by some of an unexpected bankruptcy, by others of a turtle feast; is sometimes provoked by importunate enquiries after the white bear, and sometimes with praises of the dancing dog" (5:14). Subsequently, Johnson describes how the famous fall into obscurity. He imagines their names crowded on the edge of a cliff in a debased and farcical scene: every time a new name is dropped into the crowd, one of the ones on the edge falls off.

These authors are all rejected unintentionally. But the public that rejects them is careless for reasons beyond its control. In this essay, everyone suffers, but no one is at fault. The crowd's attention is scattered; that is, it is directed only, and necessarily, to immediate concerns. So public neglect is doubly impersonal: unintentional and uncontrollable. It is in a sense gentler than deliberate rejection since it does not reflect upon the person who suffers by it, but it is also more comprehensive and radical. It spares the person, but it neutralizes the whole logic of the personal, meaning the logic that tells us that power gives one person an advantage over someone else (for example, a serious pamphleteer over a dancing dog), and that actions arise out of our intentions. In a crowd, these rules do not apply.

Johnson writes about the pamphleteer's instinctive attempt to personalize the neglect to which the crowd has subjected him; and this raises the problem of how moral action fits into the crowd. The pamphleteer comes to believe that the public has ignored his writing because they are not cultivated enough to understand him, and because his "enemies" have "been industrious, while his performance was in the press, to vilify and blast it" (5:15). We know that the public has ignored him because of pressures taking up their attention; they have not failed to understand him, they have not listened to his enemies; they have simply not noticed that he exists. This explanation he cannot bear: public stupidity, the treachery of rivals, any personally comprehensible relation to the crowd, no matter how vicious, is better than the neutrality of a purely impersonal relation.[18] "There is nothing more dreadful to an author than neglect, compared with which reproach, hatred, and opposition, are names of happiness" (R 2, 3:13). Johnson finds the pamphleteer's defensive preening ridiculous, but he also suggests that it is universal: "By such arts of voluntary delusion does every man endeavour to conceal his own unimportance from himself" (5:15). If every man uses such arts of delusion, it would seem to be because he finds himself in a crowd; the generalization echoes the view of *Rambler* No. 99 that a man guided by general benevolence alone would find himself "evaporating" amidst the multitudes of Babylon and London. Distinctions have to be made, smaller organizations have to be formed, or he will abandon himself to the fluctuations of chance. In a crowd, we have to fabricate a sense of the personal.[19] And conversely, a crowd might make us sense how the personal has been fabricated for us. In *Rambler* No. 146, we feel this in the paranoia of the pamphleteer's fantasy about enemies.

The theoretical question, the one that concerns moral action and reflection, is about how clear a distinction there is between the pamphleteer's art of delusion and the art necessary to "cantonise." Both are forms of defense against the crowd; both repress the dispiriting adumbration of the crowd's impersonal power. Might they not both affect Johnson on this account as forms of evasiveness? He comically deflates the pamphleteer in *Rambler* No. 146; might he not turn the same comic attention onto the construction of friendships—and moral reflections, inasmuch as they belong to private life, to "domestick privacies . . . where men excel each other only by prudence and by virtue" (R 60, 3:321)—and might he not particularly expose their defensiveness and artifice?

It is true that Johnson does not simply run together the pursuit of fame and the world of private cares and friendships. He contrasts "domestick privacies," for instance, with the "performances and incidents" that produce "vulgar greatness"; and in general we think of Johnson as an advocate for the special, unacknowledged dignity of lives lived in obscurity. Private life and spectacle are certainly different; and it is natural to satirize the vanity of the desire for public renown where it would seem odd or churlish to ridicule domestic life. But against the background of the crowd, the background of *Rambler* Nos. 99 and 146, it is not so easy to see that contrast. The point of the story of the pamphleteer is that he is *not* vain, and that it would make no difference if he were. To the "vulgar greatness" he seeks, the alternative is not a modest private life; the alternative is what it appears to be for the crowds in *Rambler* No. 99, that is, "oblivion." And in all of Johnson's essays on the desire for fame, he argues not that it would be wiser to enjoy the small pleasures of private life, but that those who try to become famous end up in the misery of oblivion.

Richard Sennett argues that in eighteenth-century London there was no clear distinction, at least in public places—parks, streets, theaters—between personal comportment and spectacular performance. Dress, manner, coiffeur were coded by public convention. Feeling was expressed, in Sennett's word, "impersonally." The body became a "mannequin": an occasion to display a sumptuous dress, a politically significant beauty mark, a wig representing a famous sea battle. According to Sennett, the spectacular artifice of eighteenth-century manners in everyday life warded off the threat of disorientation posed by the explosive and chaotic growth of the city. In public, people opted for spectacle so as to avoid psychic disintegration.[20] Sometimes this seems to be the alternative Johnson too finds in the crowds in the streets. In *Rambler* No. 179, he writes a little as if the people in the streets who were not showy and affected were poor, sick, and crippled:

> He that stands to contemplate the crouds that fill the streets of a populous city, will see many passengers whose air and motion it will be difficult to behold without contempt and laughter; but if he examines what are the appearances that thus powerfully excite his risibility, he will find among them neither poverty nor disease, nor any involuntary or painful defect. The disposition to derision and insult is awakened by the softness of foppery, the swell of insolence, the liveliness of levity, or the solemnity of grandeur; by the sprightly trip, the stately walk, and the lofty mien; by gestures intended to catch the eye, and by looks elaborately formed as evidences of importance. (5:177–78)

It is important to look at a crowd to see such affectation not just because a crowd offers so many specimens of humanity, but because it encourages affectation as an anxious means of displaying personal "importance." In *Rambler* No. 53, where Johnson sees no affectation in the crowd, he finds instead visages harrowed by anxiety like the poor and crippled he mentions above: we "see the streets thronged with numberless multitudes, whose faces are clouded with anxiety, and whose steps are hurried by precipitation, from no other motive than the hope of gain; and the whole world is put in motion, by the desire of that wealth, which is chiefly to be valued, as it secures us from poverty" (3:285).

The alternative is clearest when he writes less empirically and more in the vein of moral reflection; but he verges on amorality in doing so:

> Those who are oppressed by their own reputation, will per-haps not be comforted by hearing that their cares are unneces-sary. But the truth is, that no man is much regarded by the rest of the world. He that considers how little he dwells upon the condition of others, will learn how little the attention of others is attracted by himself. While we see multitudes passing before us, of whom perhaps not one appears to deserve our notice, or excites our sympathy, we should remember, that we likewise are lost in the same throng, that the eye which happens to glance upon us is turned in a moment on him that follows us, and that the utmost which we can hope or fear is to fill a vacant hour with prattle and be forgotten. (R 159, 5:84–85)

In a crowd, then, a person has virtually no past or future; a sense of inconsequentiality empties out experience. We have nothing either to hope or fear; experience is essentially visual, and we become mere images. This is a version of the "oblivion" of *Rambler* No. 146 and the "evaporation" of *Rambler* No. 99. The alternative to it seems to be only the foppery and affectation derided by *Rambler* No. 179. In this corrosive frame of mind, Johnson finds everything and every-one affected. The amorality of the last line, which pushes the con-ventional moral topic of vanity beyond its normal bounds toward nihilism, is comprehensive and eager, as if Johnson were relishing the bleakness of the predicament he describes: "the utmost which we can reasonably hope or fear is to fill a vacant hour with prattle"—

that is, not only the hour of a social engagement, but of a whole lifetime.

Sometimes Johnson speaks of oblivion as if holding it up as a grim truth, a memento mori, in this case a reminder of the crowd's obliteration of the person. His well-known remark about Ranelagh has this tone:

> When I first entered Ranelagh, it gave an expansion and gay sensation to my mind, such as I never experienced any where else. But, as Xerxes wept when he viewed his immense army, and considered that not one of that great multitude would be alive a hundred years afterward, so it went to my heart to consider that there was not one in all that brilliant circle, that was not afraid to go home and think; but that the thoughts of each individual would be distressing when alone. (*Life* 3:199)

We know that Johnson considers friendship a protection against the despair of "Babylon and London." Where are the friendships in this meditation? Why does Johnson imagine everyone going home alone? As in other passages, he imagines here an alternative between spectacle and loneliness; and the pleasures of friendship in this case seem to belong to the former. Sociability here sounds theatrical. The visitors form a crowd in which they feel slightly giddy: "expansion" could be the first stage of "evaporation." And they moderate their giddiness by submitting to the conventions of the prevailing spectacle. But as Johnson tells the story, the scene is a distraction from the real loss of bearings, the isolation at the end of the evening when one is prey to thoughts—often he speaks of crowds of thoughts—and vulnerable to circumstance. In *Rambler* No. 99 he writes of the necessity of some defense against such loneliness; here, he seems more preoccupied with the thought that the defense is a kind of evasion, and the thought is potent enough to wreck his evening.[21] (He seems also to be wishing his own loneliness in the crowd upon them. To that extent, he is apparently trying to save his evening.)

Johnson's own domestic life was only just barely distinguishable from living on the street. He never liked to go home; but he never made his house a place he could want to go home to. He was, like Richard Savage, an eternal guest. Even when he was married, he lacked a household. He visited his wife in Hampstead—by the end of her life he was not allowed to share her room—and the rest of the time he lived in temporary lodgings in London. He was nocturnal; he walked the streets at night, and sometimes stayed out till morning. When his wife died, he put together the household of outcasts who made his home into a shelter. They personified homelessness: the prostitute Poll Carmichael, whom Johnson carried home on his back after finding her lying in the street; Levet, the unlicensed "doctor" who peregrinated around London every day, and, like Johnson, stayed out till late at night—he moved in after his marriage with a streetwalker fell apart; and Anna Williams, the penniless blind woman whose father had died in the misery of the Charterhouse. These inmates, together with the freed slave Francis Barber, who several times ran away, and a former friend of Johnson's wife, lived in violent acrimony together. Occasionally Johnson brought home other strays and derelicts.

Many commentators have been moved by the moral loftiness of Johnson's charity toward these people. He gave here an instance of how "men excel one another [in private life] only . . . by virtue."[22] But in the context of Johnson's remarks on the crowd, his charity is striking for the spareness with which it dramatizes the struggle for protection against the "boundless evaporation" of living on the street. Johnson's household was only just barely a shelter, only just barely not exposure to the crowd. The household did not elaborate its privacy as an alternative world, a small society within the larger society; it only offered wanderers a place to rest while wandering. The morality of charity appeared here as the barest of comforts, only minimally differentiated from chaos and despair.

Perhaps some distaste for the consolations of spectacle, some severe determination to face the crowd's memento mori, prodded Johnson to order his private life in this way. Sometimes he seems to have wanted to startle his friends with the view of his ghastly, poignant home. Lyle Larsen observes that, even by the squalid standards of eighteenth-century London, "Johnson's personal habits—

the filthy rooms, the dirty clothes, the unwashed hands—dismayed people entering his household and viewing his private life for the first time."[23] To some extent, this effect was surely unintentional. Johnson says that home tempted him to fall apart: "The amusements and consolations of langour and depression are conferred by domestick companions, which can be visited or called at will, and can occasionally be quitted or dismissed, who do not obstruct accommodation by ceremony, or destroy indolence by awakening effort. Such society I [have] with Levet and Williams" (Larsen 84). But he also willfully dragged the sordidness of his home life into his friends' attention. He regaled the Thrales with stories of the feuding in a tone of weird bravado and irony. "Madam," he said one evening to Mrs. Thrale, "she [Miss Williams] does not like [the others] at all; but their fondness for her is not greater. She and Desmoulins quarrel incessantly; but as they can both be occasionally of service to each other, and as neither of them have any other place to go, their animosity does not force them to separate" (ibid., 83). He went on to observe that "general anarchy" prevailed in the kitchen; that he had been told so by Levet, "a brutal fellow, but I have a good regard for him." Johnson could not roast meat properly because there was no jack in the kitchen. Then "assuming a look of profound gravity he said, 'I have some thoughts of buying a jack, because I think a jack is some credit to a house.' 'Well, but you'll have a spit, too?' 'No, sir, so; that would be superfluous; for we shall never use it; and if a jack is seen, a spit will be presumed'" (83). He was concerned to keep up appearances, but he wanted his friends to laugh at his attempts to do so, to sympathize in a comic spirit with his hapless floundering among domestic squabbles.

Johnson offered his house as a parody of domesticity, and there seems to have been some aggressiveness in this. Boswell reports that, when Johnson invited guests home for tea, he had Miss Williams serve as hostess, even though, being blind, she disgusted them by sticking a finger in the cups to tell when they were full (*Life* 2:99). She also ate with her fingers. Joseph Baretti dined with Johnson as rarely as possible, for he "hated to see the victuals paw'd by poor Mrs. Williams, that would often carve, though stone blind" (*Life*

2:99). Boswell, too, declined to eat Easter dinner one year, "my stomach being so delicate that I could not bear Mrs. Williams's cookery and *finger-feeding*."[24] Sometimes Johnson carried Mrs. Williams to his friends' houses, and there, again, "from her manner of eating in consequence of her blindness, she could not but offend the delicacy of persons of nice sensations" (*Life* 3:26). Johnson was acting out of a desire to help her, entertain her, and show her respect; perhaps out of an obliviousness to his friends' distaste; but perhaps, conversely, out of a mischievous desire to discountenance them and upset the decorum of their domestic routine. He was not above regarding his tenants' squalid lives with a certain cruel levity. "During heated disputes he would sometimes act as a rooting section cheering on the underdog," writes Larsen. " 'Today Mrs. Williams and Mrs. Desmoulins had a scold,' he wrote, 'and Williams was going away, but I bid her *not turn tail*, and she came back, and rather got the upper hand' " (74). On the one hand, it was cruel to expose in this way a blind and penniless outcast like Anna Williams to an extravagantly wealthy society lady like Mrs. Thrale; on the other hand, Johnson seems to have wanted to keep reminding the Thrales, along with himself, of the squalor they could not see at Streatham. In the same way, he fiercely chastised Mrs. Thrale for complaining about the dust on the roads: "I cannot bear (replied he, with much asperity and an altered look), when I know how many poor families will perish next winter for want of that bread which the present drought will deny them, to hear ladies sighing for rain, only that their complexions may not suffer from the heat, or their clothes be incommoded by the dust;—for shame! leave off such foppish lamentations, and study to relieve those whose distresses are real" (Piozzi 219).

Some passages from the *Lives of the Poets* suggest, too, that Johnson finds something emasculating in domestic life, especially as a form of spectacle. In his view the two masters of domestic life in literature, Pope and Addison, were disposed to their topic partly because of their frailty.[25] Addison was unsuited to public business because of his shyness, Pope because of his physical infirmity. Both seem dainty in their preoccupation with elegance of manner and appearance. (Johnson says that Addison's political career fell apart because he was constantly losing time in quest of fine expressions.) The women in their lives represent an aristocratic form of domesticity steeped in spectacle and public attention. Johnson presents them as icons of debility; it is as if domestic life not only attracted the men because of their frailty, but also somehow induced the frailty. Addison's aristocratic wife, we are told, treated him in the manner of a Turkish princess who is given a husband to use as a slave (*Lives* 2:110). Immediately after this account, Johnson describes the collapse of Addison's political career (*Lives* 2:111). Similarly, Martha Blount seems to preside over Pope's death. Johnson says that she and Pope had known each other intimately for years; but he introduces her only at the biography's conclusion, at the moment when she scoffs cruelly at Pope's coming death, so that the poignant evocation of their intimacy merely measures the viciousness of her betrayal, and, more generally, the treachery of such friendship as a foundation for happiness (*Lives* 3:189–90).

The most sympathetic domestic figure in the *Lives* is Swift's companion Stella. With her, domesticity is devoid of spectacle and directed toward oblivion. The portrait focuses on the contrast between Stella's charm and the impersonality of Swift's political career. Stella was beautiful and intelligent, but quiet and retiring. Swift relied on her; but his public life took him away from her. To keep her under his control without binding himself to her in his turn, he privately acknowledged her as his wife but insisted that they live apart and that their contract remain secret. Johnson does not explain this humiliating treatment; he uses his account of it only to highlight the strand of heartlessness in Swift's political careerism. At the end, after the account of Stella's death, he writes as if Swift precipitously disintegrated—he lost his friends, his eyesight dimmed, he contracted hideous boils, and he went insane—but meanwhile his political success chugged senselessly on. "After the death of Stella, his benevolence was contracted, and his severity exasperated; he drove his acquaintance from his table, and wondered why he was deserted. But he continued his attention to the publick . . . and nothing fell from his pen in vain" (*Lives* 3:43).

Later, when he was mad and nearing death and the public prepared bonfires to celebrate his birthday, he broke his silence to say: "It is all folly; they had better let it alone" (*Lives* 3:49).

The sense of this is sentimental. Johnson is saying that no amount of public success can compensate for a loveless private life. The depiction of Stella, one of Johnson's rare excursions into the sentimental style, reinforces the message. She is treated with a pitying and tender condescension. Three times in four pages she is "poor Stella" and once she is "the unfortunate Stella." Johnson summarizes her story in sentimentalism's language of mingled didacticism and romantic extremity: "Beauty and the power of pleasing, the greatest external advantages that woman can desire or possess, were fatal to the unfortunate Stella" (*Lives* 3:40–41).

But Johnson also writes as if Swift's domestic unhappiness were somehow a punishment for his political success. His success provokes an excited response from Johnson, who sounds simultaneously admiring, envious, and dismayed. After the *Drapier* letters, Swift "gained such power as . . . scarcely any man has ever enjoyed"; he was "the oracle of the traders, and the idol of the rabble"; the "Drapier was a sign; the Drapier was a health" (*Lives* 3:36). "Nor did he much scruple to boast his influence; for when, upon some attempts to regulate the coin, Archbishop Boulter, then one of the Justices, accused him of exasperating the people, he exculpated himself by saying, 'If I had lifted up my finger, they would have torn you to pieces' " (*Lives* 3:37). The *Lives* repeatedly take pleasure in seeing presumptuous political hopes come to nothing; and according to *Milton,* there is "merriment" in seeing the contrast between "great promises" and "small performance" (*Lives* 1:98). Swift's success must have felt disconcerting to Johnson; there is scarcely anything like it elsewhere in the *Lives* or Johnson's other writings. (*Prior* comes closest.) Accordingly, one hears a note of eagerness in the paragraph that follows the account of Swift's success: "But the pleasure of popularity was soon interrupted by domestic misery. Mrs. Johnson [for the moment she is not 'Stella'], whose conversation was to him the great softener of the ills of life, began in the year of the Drapier's triumph to decline; and two years afterwards was so wasted with sickness, that her recovery was considered as hopeless" (*Lives* 3:37). The neatness and spareness of the irony moralizes the passage; it is as if Swift's pride had taken a deserved fall. By the same token, Stella seems not merely a victim of Swift's political career but also the cause of its eventual bankruptcy. Like Mrs. Addison and Martha Blount, she incarnates a spirit of decline. If she is more sympathetic than they are, it is because she represents a form of domestic life without spectacle: anonymous privacy opposed to the vain parade of Swift's public life. When she asserts her rights, she does it as an agent of oblivion.

If Johnson could be testy about the consolations of "domestick privacies," one wonders about his view of the virtues that go with them. Is there a sense in which he regarded moral maxims too as a defense against the crowd, against its logic and dissipating effects—a necessary defense but a kind of evasion?

Rambler No. 145, the one he wrote just before the number about the paranoid pamphleteer, is helpful here: it shows him at his most transparently wishful. It is about the virtue of resignation and how it enables one to be content to be a face in the crowd. Along with it come Christian humility and a whole hierarchical political view. These are values Johnson always espoused; but the essay is distinctive because in it they seem so clearly valued for the reassurance they offer; and it highlights, by contrast, how rigorously the next number, the pamphleteer sketch, takes that reassurance away. *Rambler* No. 145 is about a topic that would easily awaken Johnson's wish for some consolation: hack writing. In it, he does something unusual, namely he talks about being a hack writer as if it might somehow be a *happy* occupation. Its happiness is of a dubious sort—more a kind of insensibility. Hack writers are content to be powerless drudges, to perform the lowliest and most mechanical literary work, because, Johnson suggests, they have no inner life to speak of. They do their work and just forget about it, untroubled by imaginary aspirations regarding "posterity" or unpredictable and unreliable impulses of genius.

The authors whom I am now endeavouring to recommend have been too long 'hackneyed in the ways of men' to indulge a chimerical ambition of immortality; they have seldom any claim to the trade of writing, but that they have tried some other without success; they perceive no particular summons to composition, except the sound of the clock; they have no other rule than the law or the fashion for admitting their thoughts or rejecting them; and about the opinion of posterity they have little solicitude, for their productions are seldom intended to remain in the world longer than a week. (5:11)

For Johnson the virtue of humbleness almost always involves a bitter resignation to the misery of being unknown; and this particular *Rambler* essay begins by asserting that the bulk of mankind "must," as he says, "be content" to form the base of the pyramid of subordination and support "all that is splendid, conspicuous, or exalted" (5:9). This sense of grim resignation and grudging acceptance is so consistent in Johnson that the figure of the happily insensible and machinelike hack writer appears here in a wistful light; he is a figure out of a fantasy.

The fantasy is not simply that insensibility can make you happy with subordination, but, more deeply, that the structure of subordination can give a happy significance to your obscurity and dehumanized powerlessness. This role of subordination is apparent in two ways. First, it appears in the comparison Johnson makes between hack writing and manual labor. Manual labor, in Johnson's presentation, produces what economists call use value: it satisfies natural needs. But hack writing produces what they would call exchange value: Johnson links it with the transient movement of signs—"fashion," the "clock," and "these papers of the day, the *Ephemerae* of learning." The analogy between these ostensibly opposed activities is possible because of the pyramid of subordination, which puts them both at the bottom. But supposedly natural need determines the layout of this pyramid: those who propose new ways to satisfy needs become powerful and famous; the rest carry out the plans of the inventors and the rulers. If, then, the hack writer can be aligned with the manual laborer, the "sound of the clock" and the "fashion," which govern his work, slide over into the category of natural need, and exchange value starts to feel stabilized by the idea of use value. Then impersonality—for instance the impersonality of the clock and fashion—finds a ground in the personal; and marginality is transformed into humbleness—one's little corner of the pyramid.

As a structure of subordination, the literary world is personally manageable. This is the second way that subordination makes obscurity and powerlessness happy. Johnson here imagines that the writing scene is like a theater or a public forum. It is as if it took the form of a deliberative body. In the public sphere, people become famous or not according to laws of rational judgment. Thus, the refusal of fame to workers "is by no means contrary to reason or equity" since manual labor is not of equal esteem with intellectual labor, Johnson writes, "in the consideration of rational beings" (5:9). Johnson defends the class of hack writers as if his readers were deliberating together on a case, like jurors at a trial. In his summation, he carefully isolates the treatment hack writers deserve—"kindness" though not "reverence"—as if we will patiently apply these instructions in future deliberations. The essay's last paragraph suggests that Johnson sees himself as specifically addressing the authors of London, and urging them, as in a council meeting, to refrain from attacking the "meanest of their fraternity." "Since no man, however high he may now stand, can be certain that he shall not be soon thrown down from his elevation by criticism or caprice, the common interest of learning requires that her sons should cease from intestine hostilities, and instead of sacrificing each other to malice and contempt, endeavour to avert persecution from the meanest of their fraternity" (5:12). The passage is in the third person, and Johnson is not directly speaking to the assembly of writers; but still the passage tacitly assumes that Johnson could in fact call a session of the writers of London. They are not only a coherent body but even in a figurative sense a political one—one with interests of state and a history of military struggles—and it is as if their state were to be governed by decree: "the common interest of learning," Johnson says, "requires" that civil conflict should cease. Here, then, the model of subordination not only enables the powerless to seem to have a meaningful place in the structure of power, but also enables the writer to seem to assume the power of a moral and political authority. Shaftesbury might say that Johnson here seeks the pleasure of "cantonisation." Authors now "view the whole compass and extent of their community, and see and know particularly whom they serve, and to what end they associate and conspire."

But what if it doesn't make sense to think of the literary world as a public forum? In the next *Rambler* essay, Johnson suggests that it doesn't. This is *Rambler* No. 146, the sketch about the pamphleteer who cannot bear to acknowledge the crowd's impersonality. The essay points to an abysmal gap between the personal and the impersonal, the public and the private. For us, Johnson's tone is the key thing: he laughs at attempts to bridge this gap; and by implication, at his own political and moral rhetoric in the preceding essay. People are marginal, their subordination happens for no good reason; lives are meaningless in such ways that we cannot redeem them by thinking of society as a pyramid.[26]

The essay's irony is directed against the pamphleteer's quasi-paranoid attempt to recover a sense of the self's meaningfulness when it has been staggered by the impersonal. He is an easy target. But another way, perhaps just as ridiculous, to redeem the personal is the tactic Johnson himself employs in the preceding *Rambler* essay: the tactic of having recourse to the literary tradition of the vanity of human wishes, the literature that thrives on the self's helplessness by taking it as a sign of the transcendent power of some authoritative other, like custom, the political system of subordination, and religious truths. Johnson does not ridicule this tradition. But he makes it the object of a wistful kind of humor. After the farce about the pamphleteer, Johnson shifts into a sermonizing mode.[27] As in *Rambler* No. 145, the sermon's lesson is the importance of learning to be resigned and humble. It begins: "By such arts of voluntary delusion does every man endeavour to conceal his own unimportance from himself." But as the passage develops, Johnson underscores the theatrical mournfulness of this style to comic effect. The style is affected, and Johnson seems both to indulge it wistfully and to laugh at it.

To appreciate this humor, it is important first to note that he does not propose an alternative style to his sermonizing mode, one that would more adequately represent the mechanical impersonality of the crowd. But there is a probabilistic and quasi-sociological dimension to his writing here, which nods at the language and method of contemporary social theory. He evokes the figure of laboring "mankind" as an economic abstraction, a figure defined as an abstract impulse to satisfy immediate wants; he describes the names of the famous displacing one another in a probabilistic fashion that calls to mind ball bearings in a random motion machine; and he uses a low-level mathematical language of proportionality and measurement to represent the relation of individuals to the crowd, a language which, after eighteenth-century social theory, was to lead to demographic summaries, poll-taking, and probabilistic patterns generated by repetition. Johnson proposes none of this as an alternative, though demographic analysis would represent the movement of crowds without asserting, as *Rambler* No. 145 tries to do, a meaningful continuity between that movement and the experience of individual people. Johnson evokes both that style—the language of bureaucratic depersonalization—and the sermonlike universalizing style of the preceding *Rambler* essay, but instead of embracing either, elects to wobble indeterminately between them. For instance, in the following passage, which presents in a modified statistical terminology the effects of crowds on individuals, but which also calls to mind the traditional moral category of "vanity," as if the issue here were man's place in the cosmos:

> It is long before we are convinced of the small proportion which every man bears to the collective body of mankind; or learn how few can be interested in the fortune of any single man; how little vacancy is left in the world for any new object of attention; to how small extent the brightest blaze of merit can be spread amidst the mists of business and of folly; and how soon it is clouded by the intervention of other novelties. (5:15)

This writing conjoins two contrasting modes: Walter Benjamin might call them the rhetoric of the "aura" and the rhetoric of the "shock experience." When their incompatibility is sufficiently well marked, the result is a kind of bleak humor, a humor concerned not with humility but with unregenerate marginality. In other words, the pathos of humility comes to seem comically theatrical, not because it overdramatizes how low one has sunk, but because there is a ghastly condition in which you can sink so low that even pathos accords you too much dignity—that is, the banal helplessness of being just a face in the crowd.[28] This kind of comic theatricality is audible in the following passage:

> It seems not to be sufficiently considered how little renown can be admitted in the world. . . . Engaged in contriving some refuge from calamity . . . [the generality of mankind] seldom suffer their thoughts to wander to the past or future; none but a few solitary students have leisure to enquire into the claims of antient heroes or sages, and names which hoped to range over kingdoms and continents shrink at last into cloisters or colleges.
>
> Nor is it certain, that even of these dark and narrow habitations, these last retreats of fame, the possession will be long kept. (5:16)

Thus Johnson comically, self-consciously savors his own mournfulness. And he can savor it because its solemn, universalizing resonance—the plangency of "these dark and narrow habitations, these last retreats of fame," the melodramatic extremity of mankind "contriving some refuge from calamity"—is crazily at odds with the bureaucratic dreariness of the process of decay Johnson is writing about, the decay of the famous into the condition of an unread entry in a library catalog.

He laughs at the redemptive "cantonising" rhetoric that produces the conservative political fantasy spun out in *Rambler* No. 145, and that positions him there as a moral authority. But the feeling behind this comedy is that he emerges not with another general perspective—in particular, with the amoral perspective of social theory—but rather with the incommensurability between the personal and the impersonal—that is, with one's abysmal individual insignificance. Johnson thinks that one has got to accept this abysmal predicament; but he always writes nonetheless in the voice of a traditional moralist, a purveyor of maxims for the regulation of personal behavior. It remains to be seen how he writes his moral essays, given the skepticism which his writing about crowds induces. In *Rambler* No. 146, at any rate, he resigns himself to the thought of personal insignificance but he does it with some friction: by comically savoring the bitterness of marginality, as opposed to simply adopting the language of bureaucratic impersonality, he marks the cost of his resignation.

Two

Periodical Moralizing

Johnson was in some ways particularly disposed to be affected by crowds. As a migrant from Lichfield he must have felt daunted by London's size and confusion. Because of his disfiguring scars and convulsive twitching, he had been a misfit in Lichfield; Richard Holmes suspects that his loneliness magnified his sense of London's impersonality.[1] Alvin Kernan points out, too, that his partial blindness set him at a distance from his circumstances, so that the figures around him seemed to loom up ominously (*Samuel Johnson and the Impact of Print*, 131).

It is hard to say to what extent Johnson's profession as a writer called up to him the image of crowds. According to Richard Schwartz, the community of writers in London at that time was small. "If one remembers that perhaps 75 percent of London's population consisted of the faceless poor, we have a literary and intellectual environment which is very small and interlaced" (*Daily Life in Johnson's London*, 6). Certain neighborhoods were familiar for their literary associations; and authors "often lived in close proximity to one another and in close proximity to their publishers" (6). It seems to have been easy, by visiting coffeehouses like Button's, to meet established authors. Johnson probably met Savage through Edward Cave, or he might have run into him simply walking through the streets near Cave's offices. Cave himself, along with other prominent editors, provided a natural starting point for a struggling author like Johnson trying in the late 1730s to place himself in London.

On the other hand, Johnson himself believed that the number of writers for hire was large. "The authors of London were formerly computed by Swift at several thousands, and there is not any reason for suspecting that their number has decreased" (R 145, 5:10). He supposes the present age might be styled the "Age of Authors"; "for, perhaps, there never was a time, in which men of all degrees of ability, of every kind of education, of every profession and employment, were posting with ardour so general to the press."[2] Publishers multiplied rapidly in the eighteenth century and needed copy. By 1790 London had fourteen morning newspapers; and where there had been no provincial papers in 1700, by 1760 there were thirty-five (Porter 234). In 1695, when Parliament allowed the Licensing Act to lapse, only twenty printing houses were permitted to operate in all of England; by 1785 there were 124 printers in London alone (Kernan 59).

There is some debate as to how much literacy spread. Richard Altick believes that "by 1780 the national literacy rate was scarcely higher than it had been during the Elizabethan period" (qtd. in Kernan, 69); but Kernan says that subscription lists to lending libraries, book clubs, serial publications, and newspapers point to widespread reading (69). Roy Porter writes: "Literacy rates were gently rising. . . . Almost all males from the middle class and above were literate, but little more than half the population of labouring men (women were proportionally less literate)" (167).

Two features of what Kernan calls "print culture" probably specifically prompted Johnson to think of crowds. First, as a hack writer in the 1740s, and even into the 1750s, Johnson provided much copy, in the form of prefaces, digests, and translations, in which his aim was to be invisible. He was required merely to facilitate the presentation of someone else's work. The entrenchment of print in the eighteenth century fostered a whole class of writing of this sort; and Johnson seems to have felt strongly its emotional charge, both positively and negatively. Throughout this period he wrote anonymously. Judging from his incessant essays on the futility of desiring fame, and from his Beckett-like conception of himself, in the "Preface" to the *Dictionary,* as a lowly drudge, he repined at his anonymity as a dreary burden and humiliation. Kernan points out that aristocratic writers up into the eighteenth century scorned printed publication of writing on the grounds that it was vulgar; and when they did print their work, they often did it anonymously. But Johnson seems to have had a more modern sense that printed publication marked him as a success. He published the *Dictionary* under his name; it made his name. Before then, he seems to have preferred anonymity only in that it freed him from the burden of responsibility for what he had written. Biographers point out that he toiled sluggishly and laboriously over *Irene,* which he hoped would establish his reputation in London; but he turned out the pages of his anonymous parliamentary reports at incredible speed. Anonymity was dreary, but it also freed him up, somewhat, perhaps, as the comfortable impersonal clamor of taverns did.

Kernan observes, secondly, that the economics of publishing pressured writers to turn out a continuous flow of writing. When, for example, Johnson failed to hand in some pages of the *Dictionary* according to schedule, the publisher complained to him that he was forcing the presses to stand idle. Johnson accused himself of dilatoriness and unproductiveness, in part because of the constant pressure of deadlines he lived under. For the same reason, he was capable of churning out his work with a funny indifference and casualness. According to a famous anecdote, he wrote one of his moral essays while the printer's boy waited at the door. According to another, he wrote an essay while a friend was visiting; when the friend asked to read it, Johnson refused, saying, as he sent the essay off to the printer, "You shall do no more than I have done myself." He seems to have been a little sheepish in these episodes; but it is also as if he regarded any given essay as only one chance among many, the way that baseball players think, for comfort, about how many games there are in a season. Paul Fussell argues that the pressure of the deadline was behind the improvised, temporary feeling of Johnson's moral essays.[3] They argue associatively; they contradict themselves. They are experimental: Johnson tries an idea out on one page, then tries out the reverse on the next. Because he has to say something immediately but will always have opportunity to say something more, he can afford, and is obliged, to write impulsively and in fragments. He approached the writing of *The Rambler* with great seriousness; he prayed at its commencement, as if he were devoting himself to a holy task. But his devotion followed a crowd logic: the general undertaking was gravely important, but little could be expected of any particular essay.

These are all roundabout, figurative approaches to the crowd. They may help to explain the prevalence of crowd metaphors in Johnson's writing, but they never drove him to think of the crowd as an object of extended study in the manner of social theory. He applied himself strictly to the writing of moral essays. The crowd appears in them in as roundabout and figurative a form as it took in his life. As I said before, it appears as a sort of warp in his efforts to moralize. Just as the crowd logic of repeated deadlines seems to have made individual essays feel somehow weightless, so a crowd pressure seems to have weighed on the general project of moral reflection. Social philosophy in the eighteenth century registered that pressure in the theoretical association of moral action with private life and small communities; and Johnson appears to have absorbed that train of thought. Accordingly, we will look for the crowd's pressure not so much in what social commentary Johnson wrote as in the signs of stress we find in his moral writing, especially those linked to the theme of runaway multiplication.

The general problem, following the argument of eighteenth-century social theory, is that crowds marginalize moral action; they relativize moral authority. For Johnson, as we will now see, this emerges more specifically as the problem of what the good of writing moral essays is. The crowd puts its value in question, and Johnson struggles to think of how his moral reflection might either work as a crowd phenomenon, or in some way resist the crowd's amoral power. Much of his pathos and humor comes from his willingness to entertain the suspicion that he is fighting for a lost cause. There is uncanniness too: at some point, his writing comes to seem weirdly, senselessly dogged.

It should not be assumed, though, that this persistence marked a failure to turn to the real problem—the social problem represented by crowds—as if Johnson's commitment to traditional moral thought were merely a sign that he was a reactionary. Crowds are of theoretical interest because they make it hard to say how to turn to them. We know that they are materially powerful; but they are empirically elusive. There is a sense in which a crowd is constituted just at the moment one fails to grasp it. It may be that willy-nilly one catches its image, as it were, over one's shoulder. Johnson shows a version of what that is like.

———

Many passages confirm the impression of *Rambler* No. 146 that Johnson regards moral reflection as a defense against the crowd's disorienting effects.

That impression is apparent most generally in the contrast Johnson makes between the scholar's "closet" and the "world." The closet is linked with abstraction and intellectual system-building. It is closed off from the world and from experience, and this isolation encourages the mind to elaborate chains of reasoning that conform to the scholar's taste for logical coherence. The "world," on the other hand, is overwhelmingly, chaotically multifarious, crowded not only with people but also with customs, beliefs, and perspectives. The pieces of the world, its different fashions and opinions, have come together irrationally and accidentally. They have no systematic connection to one another. "Of the fashions prevalent in every country . . . the greater part have grown up by chance, been started by caprice, been contrived by affectation, or borrowed without any just motives of choice from other countries" (A 131, 2:483). Similarly, public opinions "have been formed by accident and custom"; people "live without any certain principles of conduct" (R 180, 5:185).

Moral reflection appears in Johnson's account as an effort to rein in and order the world's multifariousness. Scholars, bringing the strictures of their rational chains of propositions, pose some resistance to the prevailing confusion—for "we know of every civil nation that it was once savage, and how was it reclaimed but by precept and admonition?" (A 137, 2:489). The world generally overpowers the scholar once he leaves his closet, however. The learning he acquires in private has no application outside the circle of his researches: "no man can become qualified for the common intercourses of life, by private meditation; the manners of the world are not a regular system, planned by philosophers upon settled principles, in which every case has a congruent effect, and one part a just reference to another" (A 131, 2:483). Solitary reflection keeps the student's mind averted from the "living world" (R 129, 4:321). If he holds onto his principles, he seems "stiff" in company, and unable "to accommodate himself to the accidental current of conversation" (R 177, 5:169). But usually he is "in haste to mingle with the multitude, and shew his sprightliness and ductility by an expeditious compliance with fashions or vices" (R 180, 5:185–86).

Johnson offers some systematic explanations for the failure of moral speculation in such cases. It need not be taken as a contingent personal failure. The world's complexity is the deep problem; it disables the effort of reflection to produce useful generalizations for guiding conduct. It prohibits the sort of thorough evaluation of alternatives that principled decisions would require. It forces us to act blindly: "for it is necessary to act, but impossible to know the consequences of action, or to discuss all the reasons which offer themselves on every part to inquisitiveness and solicitude" (R 194, 5:204). Johnson argues that the world generally assigns significance to an action according to circumstances; that is, its meaning does not inhere in the action itself. For instance, it has "always been the practice of mankind, to judge of actions by the event," so that the same motives, even the same conduct—the conduct of Caesar and Catiline, or of Alexander and Xerxes—seem to the world either noble or reprehensible depending on whether they resulted in success or failure (A 99, 2:429–31). There are works of literature whose meaning depends on circumstance and that lose their meaning when the circumstances change and are forgotten (*Lives* 1:213; A 58; I 57). According to the "Preface" to *Shakespeare,* all questions not strictly scientific, that is, all questions of judgment are in this way circumstantial; and consequently good judgment calls for familiarity with many circumstances and perspectives. The multifariousness of the "world" disconcerts moral reflection because it raises the possibility that we may misunderstand or be unable to assimilate the relation between circumstances. There are "questions diffuse and compounded" in which universal agreement is not to be expected, for as "a question becomes more complicated and involved, and extends to a greater number of relations, disagreement of opinion will always be multiplied, not because we are irrational, but because we are finite beings, furnished with different kinds of knowledge . . . each comparing what he observes with a different criterion, and each referring it to a different purpose" (A 107, 2:441).

Since it can be impossible to know all the relevant circumstances, we often mistake an action's true moral character: we live in a "state of universal uncertainty, where a thousand dangers hover about us, and none can tell whether the good that he persues is not evil in disguise" (R 184, 5:205). Gingerly, tentatively, Johnson suggests even that an action's moral character may not be fixed; it may be essentially relational; perhaps it changes as events unfold. We are at sea in a storm, he writes, in danger of delusive meteors mistaken for stars and of violent changes of wind; but these evils can sometimes change their nature and become agents of good: "it sometimes happens that cross winds blow us to a safer coast, that meteors draw us aside from whirlpools" (R 184, 5:204–5). The confusion of the storm at sea suggests not only that the observer cannot discern the relations between events, and so their moral character, but also that those relations themselves may be arbitrary. Disasters may lead to success, and kindnesses—though Johnson will not push this idea—may be followed by calamity; and if moral significance is relational, this verges on saying that a good action can turn, with the unfolding of events, into a bad one. Johnson prefers to say that the relations are ordered and rational, and that they are under the guidance of Providence however unable we are to see it; but in any case, he argues that the world does not reveal a general order in its own terms—whatever order there is comes to it from the outside, from a perspective we do not and cannot have—and so as moralists we are forced to struggle with the radical disjunction between our principles and the world's apparent confusion.

When Johnson pictures moral authority intervening into such complication, he is apt to do so in a wishful reverie. He wonders whether it might not be best, for instance, if some impersonal judges chose for us our vocations and our spouses. The "complication" of these questions is "so intricate" that usually "the decision devolves into the hands of chance" (R 19, 3:109–10). An impartial judge might cut through the doubts and considerations by disregarding personal temperament and inclination; he might intervene trenchantly and immediately where individuals, left to themselves, would entangle themselves hopelessly in qualms and second thoughts. The judge would be one "whose authority may preclude caprice, and whose influence may prejudice [his beneficiaries] in favour of his opinion" (R 19, 3:109). "I have often thought those happy" who have had the guidance of such judges, Johnson muses (3:109). He sounds wistful; it would be nice to settle so easily the complications of work and marriage. The thought of the judge's moral authority is a little idyll of paternal benevolence, a half-serious pipe dream like the one in *Rambler* No. 145 about the happy hack writer. When Johnson imagines the settlement of marriages by decree, he recollects that this was the "ancient custom of the Muscovites," somewhat as one might invoke Tahiti or King Arthur's court (R 45, 3:246). In both cases, choosing vocations and spouses, the tone betokens the strain of envisioning a serious role for moral authority, at least in the terms Johnson works with here. He does little more than wish that things were less complicated.

Rambler No. 146's note of gentle self-parody would seem naturally to suggest itself, then, to moralists facing the predicament Johnson describes; and he strikes this note in numerous places: in *Rambler* and *Idler* essays where he jokes about the moralist's pretensions to authority ("some gratify their pride by writing characters which expose the vanity of life" [I 18, 2:58–59]); in his prefaces to the *Dictionary* and to *Shakespeare,* where he whimsically describes his Sisyphean labors; and in *Rasselas,* which pokes fun at a whole range of moral counselors, including the charismatic, melancholy figure of Imlac. Self-parody, though, would seem necessarily a short-lived mode. Pretty soon, one would guess, the whole discursive game of moral reflection would come to feel played out. But not, somehow, with Johnson. One of his most striking characteristics is the doggedness with which he insists on writing in the language of admonition and resolution despite the forcefulness of his doubts about its value. In his essays he evokes the futility of moral resolutions: "I believe most men may review all the lives that have passed within their observation, without remembering one efficacious resolution" (I 27, 2:85); and he also indulges in self-parody, as in this letter from a fictitious correspondent: "Twenty years have past since I have resolved a complete amendment, and twenty years have been lost in delays. . . . I should look back with rage and despair upon the waste of life, but that I am now beginning in earnest to begin a reformation" (I 21, 2:68). This is humorous, but it seems weird too, considering that what Johnson says here must have been literally true of him. He formed resolutions in his diary for years: formed them and broke them, the same resolutions, over and over. In the Easter entry of 1761, he reflects on the failure of his resolutions with the solemnity of a tormented conscience: "I have resolved, I hope not presumptuously, till I am afraid to resolve again."[4] How was he able to keep alive for so long both his heartfelt commitment to moral reflection and his skepticism about it?

Johnson believes that moral instruction is effective when it is general and impersonal; when, for instance, it works through certain semiconscious pressures like fashion and manners, which act constantly and repeatedly. Resolutions do virtually no good, but the "trifles" of local fashions keep the "ranks of mankind . . . in order" (A 131, 2:483); the "little civilities and ceremonious delicacies" of politeness "contribute to the regulation of the world" (R 98, 4:161). Repeating such niceties is of much greater importance than formulating conscious propositions. They "grow important only by their frequency"; but by "every moment exerting their influence upon us, [they] make the draught of life sweet or bitter by imperceptible instillations" (R 72, 4:12). The moralist does not need so much to convince the reader of new truths as to join the chorus of voices reiterating the truths already known. We need more often to be "reminded than informed." The writer can help by reinforcing the habitualness of moral ideas: that is, by "contract[ing] the great rules of life into short sentences, that may be easily impressed on the memory, and taught by frequent recollection to recur habitually to the mind" (R 175, 5:160).

Here, then, against sentimentalist social theory, Johnson argues that moral instruction works in a public rather than a private setting. He insists on this function of instruction. It restores some of the authority that moral thought lost in its confrontation with the crowd. It does so at a cost, though: the most striking thing about instruction here is that it is mechanical, repetitive, only semiconscious. This is not a frame of mind to which people are willing or able to confine their thinking, or in which they might resolve moral problems of any complexity. Further, instruction of this sort seems to have little hold over individuals. It takes hold, in Johnson's view, when it works on crowds, the "ranks of mankind." It is striking that he does not try to picture it as a scene. On the contrary, it happens "imperceptibly" over a long time; it happens, as it were, when no one notices. Instruction here is a crowd phenomenon: the "ranks" order themselves—by "precept and admonition," as he says (A 137, 2:489)—but the precepts "contract the great rules of life" that have already manifested themselves in the long course of experience. When Johnson tries to picture a particular scene of instruction, he confronts the whole range of doubts discussed earlier: an action's moral character changes depending on perspective, general advice fails for want of particular application (R 87, 4:94), and resolutions work scarcely ever. Even repetition, which governs crowds so successfully, does not always keep alive a personal influence or impression. (When Nekayah, for instance, tries to preserve the memory of Pekuah by a daily ceremony, she finds her thoughts eventually starting to wander.) The conviction that societies, through instruction, are "reclaimed by precept and admonition" (A 137, 2:489) gives moralists a reason to keep working; but it is difficult to see the link between such social change and any one writer's impact on particular readers. Much of Johnson's writing wonders, accordingly, about how to understand that connection.

His tactic is to construe moral reflection as valuable precisely when there is nothing practical to be done. This gives it a bearing on individual action (as opposed to the mass action shaped by customary maxims, rituals, etc.). It appears specifically a response to, or even a metaphorical reconceptualization of, the predicament of a person overwhelmed by multiplicity.

Boundless multifariousness, he argues, is not only a trouble but a condition of possibility for moral judgment. Judgment is necessary and valuable only because possibility is limitless. Human minds are moral because they are not constrained by natural necessity.[5] They are rarely "filled with objects adequate" to them, unlike animal minds, which are "exactly adapted to their bodies"; they range to the past and to the future: "It is, indeed, the faculty of remembrance, which may be said to place us in the class of moral agents. If we were to act only in consequence of some immediate impulse, and receive no direction from internal motives of choice, we should be pushed forward by an invincible fatality, without power or reason for the most part to prefer one thing to another" (R 41, 3:223).

Johnson compares the mind's disengagement from the body's work to the scattering of matter through infinite space. The "great globes of matter are [so] thinly scattered thro' the universe" and "the hardest bodies are so porous" that, "if all matter were compressed to perfect solidity, it might be contained in a cube of a few feet"; and in like manner, "if all the employment of life were crowded into the time which it really occupied, perhaps a few weeks, days, or hours, would be sufficient for its accomplishment, so far as the mind was engaged in the performance" (R 8, 3:41). Because the mind is unoccupied, it risks corruption and "irregularity." But implicit in this reminder of how much time we waste is another point: it is good that matter has not collapsed into a cube; and it is good likewise that the mind is wasteful and idle. Moral rectitude does not imply a fixed adherence to a preset structure, but instead a certain way of negotiating a free fall through the abyss. Johnson does not advise an absolute immersion of the mind into useful work. It has to be idle sometimes. The task of self-regulation is necessary, in this view, because the mind floats in emptiness. Following rules is not like being locked into a cube, but like following a planetary orbit. There is the erratic plunging of meteors, and there is the stately procession of planets.

"Emptiness" in this sense is comparable to crowding or the conditions under which crowding is possible. It is a lack of structure; it produces the figure of scattering. The target of regulation is above all "irregularity," and, with it, psychic chaos, the futile, unproductive turmoil of being scattered: irresolution in the "boundless variety of irreconcilable judgments," the aimless pettiness of the idler who wastes his life collecting bits of experience without arriving at any conclusions, general wisdom, or decisions.[6] The language in which Johnson describes the ordinary state of our minds is akin to that in which he describes our situation in the midst of the smoke of winding city streets and the patchwork of prevailing customs: "A thousand miseries make silent and invisible inroads on mankind, and the heart feels innumerable throbs, which never break into complaint. . . . The main part of life is . . . composed of small incidents, and petty occurrences; . . . of insect vexations which sting us and fly away, impertinencies which buzz a while about us and are heard no more; of meteorous pleasures which dance before us and are dissipated" (R 68, 3:359). Both personal character and the "world" swarm with the confusion of runaway multiplication and disorder. The distinction between character and the world is itself subordinate to a primary conception of crowding as such, crowding of whatever kind. "[F]ortitude, diligence, and patience, divested of their show, glide unobserved through the croud of life" (3:359). The "croud of life" means both the city crowd and the crowd of the passions; and they are continuous with each other. Persons piece themselves together the same way crowds do, out of "insect vexations" and "meteorous pleasures": "Such is the general heap out of which every man is to cull his own condition" (3:359).

Since the precondition of judgment is mental freedom, judgment's task is not to suppress but to "regulate" the proliferation of thoughts and desires. Though we need to "select, among numberless objects striving for our notice, such as may enable us to exalt our reason" (R 78, 4:46)—that is, to suppress certain thoughts and encourage others—there can be no question of destroying our power to think and desire with boundless freedom. And in any case, according to Johnson's account of resolutions, it is almost always impossible to suppress strong thoughts and desires, especially once they have become habitual. Pressured, then, by both the principle of acknowledging mental freedom and the necessity of surrendering to its boundlessness, Johnson recommends that we "regulate" our thoughts: that we survey and register them in a regular way. We need to "restrain them from irregular motions" (R 8, 3:42); but they become "regular" by virtue of our looking at them right.

Johnson advises the reader to perform a formalized daily review. He cites Pythagoras, who recommends that one ask three questions about the day's events every night before sleep: "Where have I turned aside from rectitude? What have I been doing? What have I left undone, which I ought to have done?" (R 8, 3:45). The three questions—especially the second one, which Johnson uses twice in his essays as an opening epigraph—assume that one passes the day ordinarily in a state of semiconsciousness. One is prey to daydreams, "ideal seducers" which constantly overtake thought unawares. Thought itself is a chaotic jumble, an "incessant cogitation" whose productiveness seems to Johnson maddening and destructive. Ordinary consciousness either does not or cannot judge or direct this flood of energy. Johnson and Pythagoras suggest that thought can help itself by acting as if it came to itself as an outside agent. The questions they recommend are useful because one can ask them as if one were someone else. They break in on the usual flow of thought by following a rule that has nothing to do with spontaneous personal impulse. They are trenchant: they cut in by virtue of their brevity and their disconnection from any specific context.[7] Johnson often attacks moral system-building because of the "concatenation of causes and effects" (R 54, 3:289) it draws one into. These questions do not build a system; instead they interrupt the blind unfolding of thought in its usual course. They establish a kind of order when they are repeated every day at the same time—not a system but a habitual pattern. Johnson seems to have relied on maxims and aphorisms, for the same reason, as a trenchant form of utterance that breaks in on the concatenation of ordinary talk and imposes itself as an impersonal voice of order, a voice that "contracts the great rules of life into short sentences."

Regulated self-scrutiny should enable us to single out and suppress dangerous thoughts (R 8, 3:46); but the regularity is virtuous in and of itself. Where no real control is possible, playing at it is itself a good thing. When Johnson imagines that impersonal judges might resolve the boundless perplexity of choosing a vocation or a spouse, he does not suggest that they would resolve those questions rationally. They would not eradicate the workings of chance; they would only formalize it by taking it onto themselves and giving it an institutional setting. The virtue of regular self-examination lies, likewise, in its ceremonial formality. Its regularity charges that particular moment of the day—perhaps a particular place, too—with "aura." There are ordinary times of the day, like ordinary days of the year; and then there is this separate moment, which joins all those other predisposed hours of self-reflection to form a distinct order of time, a hermetic time out of time. Johnson advises his readers not only to perform this exercise every night, but also to continue it on special days of the year, "stated intervals of solitude" (R 7, 3:37). He regards this as an essential Christian ritual; and the intervals of solitude are stated by the church. On the other hand, Pythagoras's questions and Johnson's maxims are portable. They can be taken anywhere and pronounced at any time. They are private. They represent the effort of a private person to ritualize his life personally by imitating a church's lofty institutional voice.

Certain emotions are peculiarly suited, because of their "artificiality," to "regulation" by moral reflection. They do not concern natural needs or self-preservation. The animal appetites of thirst and hunger and the primary passions—hope and fear, love and hatred, desire and aversion—follow an internal, natural law that dictates their proper indulgence. But since these do not give the soul sufficient employment, "new desires, and artificial passions are by degrees produced" (R 49, 3:264). Such passions—avarice, vanity, ambition, envy, friendship, and curiosity, to name a few (3:265)— are not subject to a natural law, for they concern objects whose value is merely conventional: "from having wishes only in consequence of our wants, we begin to feel wants in consequence of our wishes; we persuade ourselves to set a value upon things which are of no use, but because we have agreed to value them" (3:264). Since they are not subject to natural law, we decide the proper exercise of these "adscititious" passions through moral reflection. Some of them, "as avarice and envy, are universally condemned; some, as friendship and curiosity, generally praised"; and some are to be "regulated, rather than extinguished" (3:266), because they seem both inspiring and irrational. Both the love of fame and prejudice in favor of one's country or special group belong to this class. We "regulate" them because we cannot tell "whether they tend most to promote the happiness, or increase the miseries of mankind" (3:265). Evidently the harder it is to evaluate an action or a passion according to natural law, the more necessary it is to regulate it by moral judgment.[8]

Since the question of the value of moral reflection arises when we are helpless, lonely, and lost in a crowd, the passions we would seem to need most to "regulate" are those involving distress, fear, isolation, and the like. The passion Johnson singles out as most interesting to moral reflection is sadness. Not only is it our predominant passion—we are almost always unhappy—but it is the "adscititious" passion least subject to natural law.[9] Of all the passions, it alone does not tend naturally to a resolution. "Sorrow . . . deserves the particular attention of those who have assumed the arduous province of preserving the balance of the mental constitution"; for "there is no remedy provided by nature" for sorrow (R 47, 3:253). Other passions seek their gratification in some future state, in the attainment of some end; but sorrow dwells on what we have no power to change. Johnson speaks specifically of our powerlessness to change the past, but helps us see how moral reflection might respond to powerlessness in general.

How does one make an end to sorrow, which does not come to an end of itself? The moral answer is: the benevolent give consolation and the suffering exercise patience. Consolation and patience are moral because they operate when there is nothing else to be done. In the absence of practical, material relief, we fabricate this other, *moral* relief. The human heart must "*make* the happiness it does not find," Johnson says at the end of "The Vanity of Human Wishes."

> Consolation, or comfort, are words which, in their proper acceptation, signify some alleviation of that pain to which it is not in our power to afford the proper and adequate remedy; they imply rather an augmentation of the power of bearing, than a diminution of the burthen. A prisoner is relieved by him that sets him at liberty, but receives comfort from such as suggest considerations by which he is made patient under the inconvenience of confinement. (R 52, 3:280)

In the case of sorrow, no "proper remedy" is available to anyone; to the "grief which arises from a great loss he only brings the true remedy, who makes his friend's condition the same as before, but he may be properly termed a comforter, who by persuasion extenuates the pain of poverty, and shews, in the style of Hesiod, that 'half is more than the whole' " (3:280–81).

Rambler No. 29, an exhortation not to fret about uncertainty, helps explain how moral reflection gives consolation. Johnson speaks here of the uncertainty of prevailing confusion, like the sea-storm of human relations he evokes in *Rambler* No. 184. "The state of the world is continually changing, and none can tell the result of the next vicissitude. Whatever is afloat in the stream of time, may, when it is very near us, be driven away by an accidental blast, which shall happen to cross the general course of the current" (R 29, 3:161). Johnson advises one always to be prepared for the unexpected. This is wisdom: "A wise man is never surprised" (3:159). But though a wise man will not submit idly to "chance, without any struggle against calamity," neither will he "harrass [his] thoughts with conjectures about things not yet in being" (3:159). How is one to maintain such a delicate balance, how prepare for the unexpected without fretting about the future? One does it by lamenting the "uncertainty of life" in "general reflections" (3:160). This form of reflection, unlike stoic denial, keeps passion alive: it is a form of sorrow. But the feeling takes refuge in generality, and flees from the danger of becoming fixated on particular images. One is to lament in general reflections but refrain from "such a desponding anticipation of misfortune, as fixes the mind upon scenes of gloom and melancholy" (3:160). Thus the passion is "regulated" by being transferred into generality; and this regulation wards off the threat of a puny, disgraceful grief, a grief of helplessness, despondency, and wretched fretfulness. (Johnson compares it to erotic humiliation: "Anxiety of this kind is nearly of the same nature with jealousy in love" [3:160].)

In both Johnson's observations about sadness and the earlier argument about runaway multiplication, a similar effort is at work: to recover a sense of personal efficacity (when nothing in fact can be done) by aestheticizing the predicament in the form of a ritual. Construing lamentation or trauma as a ritual transforms its particularity into generality. It generalizes the persons involved in the calamity, and puts the grief into a form that can be repeated, which thus dissolves its uniqueness. This effort of generalization does not eradicate the passion, but only makes it easier to bear; the effort is to "regulate" the passion and to enable one to endure it with patience. The aim of consolation is to inculcate an intensely felt general grief while dissipating the power of a particular grief.

It seems to make it easier to bear because it converts grief into wisdom, or more precisely, the sufferer into a philosopher.[10] A merely particular misery victimizes those who suffer by it; it takes them by surprise and so makes them victims of chance. Life is unpredictable, but Johnson regards surprise as avoidable and shameful. "Common minds" are astonished when they encounter death, for instance, because they "submit tamely to the tyranny of accident and . . . suffer [their] reason to lie useless" (R 78, 4:49). The wise man prompts his thoughts with every funeral he sees, not just those of his near relations. The conversion of the grief into ritual and generality allays surprise: "Every funeral may justly be considered as a summons to prepare for that state, into which it shews us that we must sometime enter" (4:49). Johnson tries to provoke a similar wisdom in the reader with a learned quotation: " 'How,' says [Quevedo], 'can death be sudden to a being who always knew that he must die, and that the time of his death was uncertain?' " (4:49).

The aim of private rituals is to sustain the feeling of grief but to translate it into a general lamentation rather than a particular one. This effort strengthens patience by removing the element of chance and absurdity from suffering. It transforms it into a form of melancholy wisdom and tragic grandeur. Since it is performed privately, though, it does not integrate the sufferer's distress into a material structure of generality—a public funeral, for example. If the deep distress is a fear of scattering, general lamentation resolves it symbolically but not materially. Johnson struggles uncomfortably with its merely symbolic generality.

When his mother died, for example, he was in the midst of writing the *Idler,* and the numbers written immediately following her death show him repeating to himself what he had written in the *Rambler* about mourning. The tone of the essays is exhausted and despondent, but also, notably, reproachful. Johnson takes this occasion to reprove the reader and himself for being surprised when death comes, as if there were something shameful in that surprise and surprise were mourning's deepest meaning. "That it is vain to shrink from what cannot be avoided, and to hide that from ourselves which must some time be found, is a truth which we all know, but which all neglect. . . . Nothing is more evident than that the decays of age must terminate in death; yet there is no man, says Tully, who does not believe that he may yet live another year" (I 41, 2:129). Then the essay goes on to insist on the regularity and universality of death. Providence uses our grief to undermine our love of life, and nature insures that those who live long must inevitably outlive those whom they love and honor. Two weeks later he wrote an essay about the parallel between the day, the year, and a lifetime. This parallel is meant to remind us, Johnson says, of the inevitability of our death. That is, death is not only inevitable but regular, almost predictable, for a lifetime has as easily recognized a pattern as the passage of a day. The particularity of a day effortlessly mirrors the generality of a whole life, and by contrast, the particularity of an individual life has the shapeliness of day in its generality. Day, year, and life pass by in order to mark the irreversibility of time: day "wastes away" into night, spring declines into winter, youth becomes age (2:136). But the sheer loveliness of the pattern in which all these units of time mingle, raising the particular to the dignity of the general, offers a consolation for the bitterness of its lesson. It incorporates death into the stately movement of a pageant.

What Johnson does not want to say just now is that his mother's death and his own mourning were just *his* problem. The most despondent moment of the two essays speaks of this: "Such is the condition of our present existence, that . . . every inhabitant of the earth must walk downward to the grave alone and unregarded, without any partner of his joy or grief, without any interested witness of his misfortunes or success" (2:130). So here the world appears as a vast community of isolates; Johnson means that we all outlive each other, but he says it in a wild hyperbole ("every inhabitant of the earth must walk . . . alone and unregarded") as if we were lost and alone in a crowd, doomed to die without ceremony, buried in an unmarked box, anonymously, among a crowd of other anonymous transients. The passage evokes the specter of a death like Richard West's, which Gray lamented because it was left to him to supply the place of general lamentation and to pretend that West's death was not just one death among others. In the eighteenth century there are a series of famous efforts on the part of writers to take the place of rituals which they feel they can no longer expect—in particular to perform their own funeral: Pope fills his own urn in the "Epistle to Dr. Arbuthnot," Gray writes his own epitaph and dreams his own funeral in the "Elegy," Clarissa gives herself her own last rites; and Johnson is writing in a similar vein in this number of the *Idler*. We know that he was trying this week to find money to pay for his mother's funeral; while he waited he wrote, among other things, this secular sermon on mourning.

Johnson's awkwardness about displaying his personal grief in the essays following his mother's death is one sign that the generality of the consolation is imaginary. Supplying by himself the elements of the ceremony, which ought to be social and institutional, involves some strain. The ceremony does not incorporate his personal grief into a larger social experience; it abstracts from it. Writing about personal problems is embarrassing. He does it apologetically: "The following letter relates to an affliction perhaps not necessary to be imparted to the publick" (2:128). This remark casts in the odd role of an alibi the institutional voice of moral wisdom that follows. He really wants to lament his private unhappiness, but since it would seem gross and lugubrious to do so explicitly, he has recourse to this dignifying ruse. Also he presents the essay as the work of a fictional correspondent. Like Gray, he both writes the sermon for his private funeral ceremony and pretends that it comes from someone else. But the sermon's lesson is that the "speculative reasoner" thinks too rarely of his own condition. He shrinks from what cannot be avoided; his thoughts "are always from home, [his] eye wanders over life, [his] fancy dances after meteors of happiness kindled by itself, and [he] examines every thing rather than his own state" (2:129). Johnson constantly prodded himself to turn his thoughts on "his own state," but here he finds himself having to do so in someone else's voice. Pretending to be someone else, he delivers a sermon to a mass readership by way of scolding himself. It is bound to be hard to consider your own state when you have to pretend at the same time to be an impersonal institutional authority.

When Johnson considers that the generality of moral reflection is merely symbolic, he doubts its value. General lamentation is supposed to bring consolation for uncertainty, but his account of the elderly suggests that such wisdom does little to strengthen moral courage in solitude. Old age's solitude recalls, again, the loneliness of Babylon and London. Johnson emphasizes that a man who has outlived his friends feels lost in a crowd. He "stands forlorn and silent, neglected or insulted, in the midst of multitudes, animated with hopes which he cannot share" (R 69, 3:365). The grave wisdom which comes then to age does not impress Johnson much. He characterizes it as a kind of *ressentiment.* When you have nothing to live for, you have recourse to sour precepts, and you begrudge youth its energy and hopefulness. Thus, youth, which is full of ardor, has nothing to do with "the cold caution, the faint expectations, the scrupulous diffidence" of experience and disappointment; and age wonders in its turn "that neither precepts, not testimonies, can cure boys of their credulity and sufficiency" (R 69, 3:365). Youth is blind and doomed, Johnson writes; but by pairing age with youth as its equal opposite number, he implies that it is blind too, blind, presumably, in imagining that its knowledge of disappointment is good for anything. In other places, Johnson is more hopeful or lyrically melancholy; but in this essay, he prefers the note of disenchantment. Knowing about misery's inevitability is worthless, even worse than worthless. It "may be doubted" whether he "that extends his care beyond himself"—and tries, among other things, to warn the young about disappointment—"does not multiply his anxieties more than his pleasures, and weary himself to no purpose by superintending what he cannot regulate" (3:366).

Johnson finds, too, that general lamentation may not only fail as a symbolic substitute for a sense of social order but may in fact deepen the mourner's estrangement. People dislike moralists and scholars because of their gloom; melancholy is a meditative virtue but not a social one. At most, people admire the scholar's severity, but as Johnson often says, people commonly do not love those whom they reverence or admire. Johnson's own gloom in *The Rambler* did not make him popular, not at the time he wrote in any case. Readers complained; they wanted something sprightlier, like *The Spectator*. Boswell quotes a long letter from a minister deprecating Johnson's gloom as unchristian (4:300–302).

The most successful medium of social commerce, Johnson writes, is not lamentation or moral brooding, but what he calls "good humour." It is the attribute of the "darlings of the world"; it is the " 'balm of being,' the quality to which all that adorns or elevates mankind must owe its power of pleasing," as Johnson writes in a letter attributed to a fictitious correspondent, telling him to lighten *The Rambler*'s tone (R 72, 4:13). But since we live most of our lives in misery, good humor is generally a deception. In company we try to deceive one another into believing that we are pleased, primarily by declining to show that we are let down: "no one will be the first to own the disappointment" (I 18, 2:58). Consequently the "public pleasures of far the greater part of mankind are counterfeit" (2:57). We are not only willing but anxious to be so deceived. We do not scrutinize the delusiveness of our pleasure; for the "general condition of life is so full of misery, that we are glad to catch delight" on any terms, however fraudulent (2:57). In other words, sociability tends to call for a certain dishonesty and theatricality. Johnson poignantly implies that there is missing a public sanction for unhappiness; to survive in public, people have to dissemble the unhappiness that they are almost always feeling. Good humor is a technique for leaving such illusions undisturbed. Good-humored people are pleasing because everything seems to please them. They confirm our best opinions of ourselves. They themselves are typically mediocre: "The darlings of the world will, indeed, be generally found such as excite neither jealousy nor fear and are not considered as candidates for any eminent degree of reputation" (R 72, 4:14). But because their mediocrity reflects a general inability or unwillingness to find fault, people love them. A good humored man is "only welcome to . . . company, as one by whom all conceive themselves admired, and with whom any one is at liberty to amuse himself when he can find no other auditor or companion, as one with whom all are at ease, who will hear a jest without criticism, and a narrative without contradiction, who laughs with every wit, and yields to every disputer" (4:15).

In the *Idler* essay written after his mother's death, Johnson adopts a fictional persona and rises into a sermonlike reflection on the obligation to remind ourselves that death is inevitable; in such anonymous and institutional tones, moral thought is allowed to dwell publicly on unhappiness. But to draw readers in as companions, the moralist has to show good humor. "Without good humour, virtue may awe by its dignity, and amaze by its brightness; but must always be viewed at a distance, and will scarcely gain a friend or attract an imitator" (4:13). The moralist's style of general lamentation offers a kind of general solace; but it is antipathetic to the solace of sociability.

Johnson wavers ambivalently between these principles. He recommends good humor as an essential grace in a moralist: "He that regards the welfare of others, should make his virtue approachable, that it may be loved and copied" (4:16). But most of his essays on good humor ridicule it for its stupidity and dullness;[11] and they evince sarcastic bitterness, too, as if Johnson felt aggrieved that love should come to placid mediocrity, while neglecting thorny greatness, "which swells the heart of the lion in the desart, where he roars without reply" (R 72, 3:13). Good humor is loud, "obstreperous," indolent, and lacking in pride (R 188, 5:223). At a club one man endears himself by turning his wig backwards, another smuts the nose of any stranger who comes in, another purrs like a cat, and another barks like a dog (5:223–24). "Such are the arts" of social amusement, Johnson writes. One is apt to "despise" them, but one is obliged not to "blame" them; "for it is not always necessary to be reverenced, but it is always necessary to be loved" (5:224). Several of the *Rambler* essays, taking a more defiant tone, indignantly complain that the social world spurns scholars and moralists out of envy of their superiority;[12] and in his farewell number Johnson defines his work as determinedly unsocial: he is proud to say that he has "seen the meteors of fashion rise and fall, without any attempt to add a moment to their duration," that he has "never complied with temporary curiosity," and that he has attended only to bare, "abstracted truth" (5:316).

Considering this antipathy between moral instruction and sociability, Johnson writes that it makes it hard to imagine books having much effect on the conduct of the "world." Clearly an individual writer "seldom works a visible effect upon cities and nations" (A 137, 2:490). The "greater part" of readers "peruse [a book] with dispositions that very little favour their own improvement": the "most general and prevalent reason of study, is the impossibility of finding another amusement equally cheap or constant, equally independent on the hour or the weather" (2:490). Such considerations have convinced some critics that to write improving works is to "fume away" time "in useless evaporations": "that to call upon mankind to correct their manners, is, like Xerxes, to scourge the wind or to shackle the torrent" (2:488). Against his argument, Johnson justifies his persistence in writing by shifting out of the language of empirical description. He will not sketch a particular scene in which the moralist can be said certainly to act in the "world."

Instead, he rests his determination to continue on the hope that, in ways he cannot control or predict, his work *might* act to good effect:

> [P]erhaps, it seldom happens, that study terminates in mere pastime. Books have always a secret influence on the understanding; we cannot at pleasure obliterate ideas; he that reads books of science, though without any fixed desire of improvement, will grow more knowing; he that entertains himself with moral or religious treatises, will imperceptibly advance in goodness; the ideas which are often offered to the mind, will at last find a lucky moment when it is disposed to receive them. (2:491)

Or again, as he says in conclusion: "For my part, I do not regret the hours which I have laid out on these little compositions. . . . I am willing to think, that many have been affected by single sentiments [in them]" (2:492).

Johnson writes here diffidently. The language of probability is natural for him since it provides a way of calculating chances according to rules; but it is anathema because of its mechanistic, amoral character. In *Rambler* No. 181, that is, in between Nos. 180 and 184 about the disabling randomness of the "world," Johnson tells about the degradation of a man who becomes obsessed with the lottery. Trying to win the lottery would be a way of dramatizing the struggle with chance; winning would be like emerging into a state of masterful self-determination. But the longer the struggle to win, the more deluded one seems: among other things, Johnson's gambler spends one week in his garret, rolling his dice 330,000 times in an attempt to figure out which number is most likely to turn up. A clergyman admonishes him at the end: "You have long wasted that time which, by a proper application, would have certainly, though moderately, encreased your fortune, in a laborious and anxious persuit of a species of gain, which no labour or anxiety, no art or expedient can secure or promote" (5:191). Johnson wants to believe in tasks to which one can "properly apply" oneself; what terrifies and fascinates him is the prospect of a world of chance which condemns one to a "laborious and anxious persuit" of what "no labour or anxiety" can attain. But if the student, entering the "world," finds that his private meditations have no application there because it has been built up by chance and caprice, then isn't his devotion to his meditations and rules like the anxious and pointless labor of the lottery enthusiast? Here is how, in the preceding *Rambler* essay, Johnson expresses his dismay that scholars grow corrupt as soon as they enter the world: "why should he whose life is spent in contemplation, and whose business is only to discover truth, be unable to rectify the fallacies of imagination, or contend successfully against prejudice and passion? To what end has he read?" (R 180, 5:185).

Johnson imagines the gambler and the moralist (the "moral speculatist") in essentially the same terms: they confront the domain of chance; like a stormy sea it allows them no power of self-direction (this metaphor for the moralist's condition appears over and over; *Rambler* No. 102 gives an extended version); and in the midst of this confusion, the moralist and gambler play at having power over chance, and their play takes the form of an apparently directed, but actually endless, pointless, crazily repetitive labor. Johnson wrote moral essays and formulated (and broke) resolutions for years: practically, it was like a man in his garret throwing the dice 330,000 times. And, in *Rambler* No. 184, about the stormy sea of chance, written a week and a half after the number about the lottery, when he writes about the essayist's subjection to chance, he describes the conclusion of his task with a gambler's excitement, fantasizing about the night his number will be the one they call. After the periodical essayist strays among a chaos of possible topics, "necessity enforces the use of those thoughts which then happen to be at hand. The mind rejoicing at deliverance on any terms from perplexity and suspense, applies herself vigorously to the work before her, collects embellishments and illustrations, and sometimes finishes with great elegance and happiness what in a state of ease and leisure she had never begun" (5:202). Here literary genius is like having a "system"; it is imagined as a way of managing randomness.

———

Rasselas, also written, famously, at the time that Johnson's mother died,[13] makes a contrast with the *Idler* essays of that period in that it treats the generalizations of moral reflection with skepticism and diffidence.[14] Those essays evince distress and a craving for solace; *Rasselas* is by comparison flinty and disillusioned.

Most of its episodes illustrate the failure of generalizing claims about the nature of life, as in the stories of the various wise men who propose schemes for the improvement of life but turn out empty (like the advocate of reason [chap. 18], the hermit [chap. 21], and the philosopher of nature [chap. 22]). At least two passages—the passages about the inventor and the astronomer—metaphorically dramatize the hope of general perspective and reject it as a fantasy. (The inventor supposes that the "fields of air are open to knowledge" [24], as if flying were an essentially philosophical position.[15]) Imlac's famous monologue about poetry and general truth is similar: he exclaims about the poet's powers of generalization ("he must disregard present laws and opinions, and rise to general and transcendental truths, which will always be the same"[44]); meanwhile, *we* see that he is succumbing to an "enthusiastic fit" (46).

The prince's monologue which opens the story is interesting because it suggests why, despite its decayed authority, moral generalization continues to exercise a fascination, over Johnson as well as us: it has imaginative appeal (rather than practical value). That monologue laments the tragedy of human desire, which seems to be driven by a "latent sense for which [the world] affords no gratification" (13); but the lamentation is itself aestheticized: the prince's voice is plaintive but his look "discovered him to feel some complacence in his own perspicacity, and to receive some solace of the miseries of life, from consciousness of the delicacy with which he felt, and the eloquence with which he bewailed them" (14). The scene with the inventor suggests that such speeches give pleasure because they gratify our desire for perspective, freedom of movement, and moral dignity. (Like the astronomer, the inventor acquires psychological depth through the notion that he restrains himself from using deep, mysterious, and destructive powers at his command.) In some passages the pleasure appears compulsive. There is a comic example in the scene where Rasselas and Imlac decide to dig a tunnel out of the Happy Valley. The plan comes to

Imlac after he sees some conies driven from their burrows. He is not content to say: "These conies give me an idea—why don't we dig a tunnel?" He says: "It has been the opinion of antiquity . . . that human reason borrowed many arts from the instinct of animals; let us, therefore, not think ourselves degraded by learning from the coney. We may escape by piercing the mountain in the same direction" (57–58). The advice is good, but how did the opinion of antiquity get in there? The circumlocution reveals a word-struck sensibility, a quixotic mind eager to find in every occasion a reminder of some loved literary experience. The elaborateness of it puts it on the verge of parody; Imlac here has something in common with figures of rhetorical excess and charlatanry like Mr. Micawber or even W. C. Fields.

But what would keep one writing in the vein of moral generalization when it failed to give pleasure, as when it seemed composed of the precepts and rules of the old man, weary of life, depicted in *Rambler* No. 69? Imlac suggests that imagination operates independently of the dictates of pleasure. Imagination is a primary drive, one which ultimately appears to be more fundamental than need or desire. At first, he argues, it seeks appeasement in the satisfaction of natural desires; when these have been gratified, it fabricates artificial desires: "[The] hunger of imagination . . . preys incessantly upon life, and must be always appeased by some employment. Those who have already all that they can enjoy, must enlarge their desires. He that has built for use, till use is supplied, must begin to build for vanity" (118). According to this scheme, imagination attaches itself parasitically to the pursuit of needs; but as the prince's opening meditation shows, imagination meddles with our sense of need and urges us to feel hungry even when we are full and makes us tired of the amusements today that entertained us yesterday (13). The imagination presents objects of desire which we do not need in order to keep itself tense and active: again, in Johnson's words, "from having wishes only in consequence of our wants, we begin to feel wants in consequence of our wishes; we persuade ourselves to set a value upon things which are of no use, but because we have agreed to value them" (R 49, 3:264). Such desires are merely an alibi for the exercise of the imagination; they reveal that all desire acts in this way to some extent.

But Imlac finds in the pyramid a sign that, at some point, imagination comes detached from desire altogether. A king builds a pyramid when his "treasures surmount all real and *imaginary wants*" (119; my emphasis). Nothing gives him pleasure (he seeks "to solace . . . the satiety of dominion and tastelessness of pleasures"). What drives him now is not desire; desire appears to have been only a means, now exhausted, of motivating or enacting imagination. That is, when gratifications fail to please the imagination, they fail to please at all: in this sense, desire is merely a form of imagination. The latter is presented, in the erection of the pyramid, as what appears to be a purposeless compulsion to repeat. The king amuses the "tediousness of declining life, by seeing thousands labouring without end, and one stone, for no purpose, laid upon another" (119).

As a compulsion to repeat, imagination might drive moral reflection to review moral maxims incessantly. This appears to be happening even in the episode at the pyramids. Imlac has encouraged the prince and princess to visit them by way of taking an opportunity really "to live." "It seems to me," said Imlac, "that while you are making the choice of life, you neglect to live" (111). The prince and princess object that the ancient past has no bearing on their present concerns, and Imlac replies that it has a greater bearing than they believe. "The present state of things is the consequence of the former"; further, it is useful to study "the progress of the human mind," especially for those "who have kingdoms to govern"; and by observing any "uncommon work," we "enlarge our comprehension by new ideas, and perhaps recover some art lost to mankind" (112–14). Imlac thus prepares the travelers for a feast of new experiences, but after taking some measurements of the pyramid, and talking (we are told in one sentence) with nearby inhabitants, the group settles down to listen to Imlac's reflections on the incessant hunger of the imagination, the theme we read about in Rasselas's first meditation, in his subsequent daydreaming, in the episode with the inventor, in Imlac's story, and in later stories. The point is not that the book is boring, but rather that it is compulsively readable; Johnson, Imlac, the prince and princess, and the reader are unable to get enough of this theme. The experiences along the way serve as occasions to repeat it. This episode particularly dramatizes how all speculation and experience keep circling back to the same conclusion. Determined to "live," eager to acquire useful knowledge, to see the development of human society with their own eyes, and to enlarge their comprehension, they fervently restate a truth they already knew. In the disparity between their intentions and the moral reflections that take up their (and the narrator's) attention, we can see a trace of imagination's compulsiveness.[16]

Three

The Vanity of Human Wishes

Readers who praise Johnson for his humanistic grasp of the inter-relatedness of general human nature and concrete personal experi-ence also argue that his rhetorical ideal is to fuse detail and abstract language. W. J. Bate writes, for example, that, in Johnson, the "craving for concrete purchase and impression" is "locked in pro-ductive conflict" with the "need and instinctive clutch for the sta-bility of generalization" (285). Neither concrete impressions nor stable generalizations, according to Bate, predominate in Johnson's writing; but neither do the differences between them undermine the writing's control and sense of formal integrity. Their conflict is productive. The vividness of his imagery deepens the emotional power of his general observations; and the comprehensiveness of his general observations intensifies the poignancy of his imagery.

The theme of the crowd obstructs the easy movement between these terms, though. The preceding chapters have tried to show that Johnson evokes a deep split between the general authority claimed by moral reflection and the relativism imposed on thought by the experience of crowds. It is hard to appreciate how a particular action illustrates the general nature of virtue when it may be that virtue does not *have* a "general nature," or only has it as an imaginary construct. By the same token, the rhetorical ideal of integrating detail and abstraction seems suspect, especially as a rule for the use of illustration. Johnson is ambivalent about moral reflection; rhetorically, one might expect signs of that ambivalence in the relation between exemplars and what they are supposed to exemplify.

"The Vanity of Human Wishes" is good to turn to for an example, since it is not only rhetorically concentrated, but also concerned with the topic of exemplarity. Critics have indirectly registered the importance of this topic in their uncertainty as to whether the poem's illustrative characters are supposed to arouse pathos or scorn. Critics point out, on the one hand, that the poem's psychological subtlety gives the portraits of Wolsey, Charles XII, and others a quality of tragic weightiness and massiveness; they exemplify the tragic insight that desire is radically insatiable and doomed to frustration. On the other hand, critics sense that the poem has a tone of sarcastic impersonality that deflates the characters; they seem not tragic but absurd; they illustrate the laughable futility of all worldly striving. Both notions sound right, I think: they describe the two sides of the poem's disjunctive structure of exemplification. Exemplary sorrow is tragic, exemplary vanity is absurd; but a sorrow that fails to be exemplary, that illustrates nothing but itself, is tragic because of its absurdity, tragic because of its untragic localness, narrowness, unresonant paltriness.[1]

The difficulty of generalization appears in the poem's most obvious and familiar formal characteristics. Both as a catalog and as an imitation of a classic Latin poem, "The Vanity of Human Wishes" raises questions about exemplarity and generalization common to many eighteenth-century poems.[2] It invites the reader to admire how the author motivates his disconnected, open-ended list, and keeps the sequence from growing stale; and it encourages the reader to enjoy the ingenious correspondences between the imitation's examples and those of the original poem, and to wonder about their significance. In some works, such correspondences mean to evoke the operation of some general principle of human behavior and in others they start up the ambiguities of mock heroic style. In Johnson's poem, the exemplars are meant to illustrate the most general principle of human life ("from China to Peru")—the fatal insistence of vanity—but they also have the mock heroic's tough, inert particularity.[3] Among their number, Johnson includes Cardinal Wolsey, Archbishop Laud, Maria Theresa, and Charles XII of Sweden, all of them figures who strongly impressed the public imagination in the eighteenth century but did so as very specific, historical personages. They were never figures of mythic proportions, only ones of enormous social importance, and the poem that depicts them does not create an effect of universal truth similar to, or at any rate in the same way as, for example, its biblical counterpart Ecclesiastes.[4] What kind of generality is it striving for instead?

A programmatic introductory couplet about affliction suggests an answer: "Fate wings with ev'ry Wish th'afflictive Dart, / Each Gift of Nature and each Grace of Art."[5] This is about affliction but also about exemplarity. Its drift is that qualities of character are always merely the means by which individuals exemplify suffering. Affliction does not arise, as one might normally assume, from frustrated desire, or from the gratification of wishes that turn out to be misguided. The couplet's view is the reverse of this. Fate throws darts of affliction: no matter what, they are going to come. Desires, in the shape of wings, are added to the darts; presumably they make them fly straight and hit their target. Affliction, therefore, is universal in the sense that it is impersonal, and desires are not its source[6] but a means by which it is given form. The idea is that everyone is bound to suffer, but that their desires determine the particular way in which people suffer. Whether the desires are gratified or not makes no difference from this point of view, though Johnson stresses in the next couplet the misery that comes from gratified desire: "With fatal Heat impetuous Courage glows, / With fatal Sweetness Elocution flows" (ll. 17–18). Here it is rather as qualities of character than as objects of desire that these virtues bring misery. They are not particularly delusive in themselves; they simply determine that, when the misery comes, it takes this form rather than that one: "Impeachment stops the Speaker's pow'rful Breath, / And restless Fire precipitates on Death" (19–20). Presumably weaknesses of character serve as wings on the afflictive dart, but Johnson stresses that strengths do too; and so it would appear that character as a whole forms those wings; and that, as such, each individual character is just a modification of suffering, one particular way among others in which an impersonal fatality is acted out.

Any individual character is an example of a general truth, the vanity of human wishes; but the example itself has no universal significance or application. W. K. Wimsatt speaks of the "concrete universal" in Romantic poetry, a figure in which general concept and particular instantiation are so intertwined and mutually defining as to be inconceivable as separate notions.[7] This would be a sense in which an example might have universal significance. Johnson's examples, as wings on a dart, are by contrast inherently incomplete; they derive their sense from a general concept to which they are externally attached; and their particularity is manifestly and irreducibly contingent. A well-known notion from Jacques Derrida helps describe Johnson's conception of exemplarity. Derrida speaks of the "supplement" which is added to a body or a text in order to complete it, but which, as an attachment, does not become fully assimilated to it.[8] Johnson presents character as a supplement to affliction. It derives its whole sense, literarily, from the latter term, to which it brings nothing but a form of expression. As exemplification, it is an ornamental addition to a general meaning: it is merely figurative. But at the same time, it is a necessary addition: the dart of affliction needs wings in order to fly straight and to hit a target. And character gives affliction a target to hit. Having character in this sense gives the dart its meaning, like a bullet with your name on it.

The notion of character as supplementary example is compatible with the general critical perception that Johnson's poem is innovative particularly because of its psychological subtlety and precision. But the more attention Johnson gives to his illustrations, the greater the chances that using them as *mere* examples will seem harsh and disconcerting. Numerous features suggest that Johnson seeks this effect of harshness, and that he thematizes it as disenchantment.

To see the tension produced by the supplementary relation between examples and generality—here, character and suffering—consider the poem's treatment of desire. Character seems perhaps most powerful and determining in the poem in its role as the agent of desire. Desire is presented as a terrifying force. It takes a lot to relegate it to the wings of affliction's dart. One measure of its terror lies in a recurrent peculiarity in the poem which arises, it appears, from Johnson's notion that desire is insatiable. Each of the poem's miniature tales follows an identical path of rising and falling (as prescribed by the line "They mount, they shine, evaporate, and fall" [76]). But oddly, none of them explains the cause of the turn of fortune. It is always a blow out of nowhere, for the reader as well as for the character. The poem does not draw a providential moral from it; it does not remind the reader that a single stroke of bad luck can destroy a life's work. Instead, the poem deliberately obscures the chain of events that lead to the catastrophe in each story. Wolsey and Xerxes are supremely powerful, but then suddenly they lose everything. The poem says of Wolsey: "At length the Sovereign frowns"; and that's that, as though it were, in the most mechanical way, just a matter of time.[9] Of Xerxes: "rude Resistance lops the spreading God." No explanation seems necessary. The comic sound of the phrase ("lops the . . . God") helps make the business seem routine and humdrum. There is more about Charles XII—the poem refers to the Russian winter, to famine, to Charles's frenzy, his failure to face reality—but the crisis does not appear, except in a dramatic break in the syntax: "He comes, not want and cold his course delay;— / Hide, blushing Glory, hide Pultowa's day" (209–10). It is as if the climax went without saying. (In Johnson's day, Charles's story was certainly well known.) But why not make more of it?[10]

The effect is interestingly different in Juvenal. He presents a similarly dramatic contrast between the exemplar's early great fortune and later downfall, but he speaks as someone weighing alternatives in the present tense, not as a storyteller. He asks the reader to compare Sejanus before and after: "You would like, no doubt, to have the pikes, cohorts and illustrious cavalry at your call, and to possess a camp of your own? . . . But what grandeur, what high fortune, are worth the having if the joy is overbalanced by the calamities they bring with them? Would you rather choose to wear the bordered robe of the man now being dragged along the streets?"[11]

This is the form, too, of Juvenal's commentary on Hannibal and Xerxes. He tells parts of their stories, but his mode is distinctly argumentative rather than narrative: he asks the reader to compare before and after and to draw the appropriate conclusion. It is true that in the Sejanus passage there is a brief interest in telling the story of the crisis: " 'But on what charge was [Sejanus] condemned? Who informed against him? . . . '—'Nothing of the sort; a great and wordy letter came from Capri.'—'Good; I ask no more' " (199). But this is inserted into an argument; unlike Johnson's Wolsey passage, it is not the climax of a passage organized as a story; and unlike the Wolsey passage, it makes clear, by its understatement, the temper behind the sovereign's frown. Johnson's imitation instead organizes Juvenal's argumentative meditation as a story. In the process, the gap between before and after, which is merely the effect of contrast in Juvenal, becomes a gap in the narrative, and it creates the sense that information has been left out or that circumstances are shifting around the characters without explanation. The effect seems quite deliberate.

The stories here are all about insatiable desire. Johnson's terseness and anticlimactic style seem responses to this theme. Insatiability is important here because it makes objects in the world—in fact all the objects in the world—seem empty and unsatisfying. They fade and evaporate. None of the characters comes across as having enjoyed his pleasures. Desire does not enhance the value or the savor of objects, it dries them out. It promotes accumulation rather than consumption. The key metaphor for it is counting:

> Great *Xerxes* comes to seize the certain Prey,
> And starves exhausted Regions in his Way;
> Attendant Flatt'ry counts his Myriads o'er,
> Till counted Myriads sooth his Pride no more;
> Fresh Praise is try'd till Madness fires his Mind,
> The Waves he lashes, and enchains the Wind . . . (227–32)

The quotation makes clear that once desire takes this form of insatiable, joyless accumulation, it becomes a terror, a kind of insanity. For Wolsey, Xerxes, and Charles, the whole world threatens to go stale; all the objects in it risk falling into the gray neutrality of items in an arithmetical sum. The dreadfulness of it makes Wolsey despair ("Still to new Heights his restless Wishes tow'r, / Claim leads to Claim, and Pow'r advances Pow'r; / Till Conquest unresisted ceas'd to please" [106–8]); and it drives Xerxes insane and Charles frantic. But then, when the crisis in their fortunes comes, the world recovers its color and variety and density. After the whole world has yielded to Wolsey's desire, at last he encounters in the king's frown an object he cannot call his own; and what Xerxes finds in the Greeks, finally, is "Resistance." The anticlimaxes of the passages make sense in these terms. The crucial action in each episode is the arrival of an object that successfully resists desire; and the anticlimactic, disjointed style of the account strips the story down so as to direct attention onto the bare fact of that arrival. The crises seem vague as parts of a story, because they feel tacked on; but as symptoms of fear, they make sense. The arbitrariness of their arrival suggests that they are wished for, like figures patched into a dream. They restore solidity to objects. In a roundabout way they restore purposefulness to desire in that they make it seem a desire for something real and specific. They seem to be therapeutic: after his downfall, Xerxes has "humbler thoughts," which apparently means that he is no longer mad.

According to D. V. Boyd, Johnson has a Pascalian sense that the mind lacks "true objects" to fill it up, and that in its despair it seizes upon the objects of the world though they are "false." Humanity is suspended between Pascal's "two infinities" and suffers from an "ontological insecurity" (388–89). The mind seizes on objects for a feeling of certainty necessary to its survival. Under the circumstances, the "mere act of survival, of maintaining one's existence, demands a considerable, even an heroic, act of will" (389). Boyd argues that this desperation drives Johnson to knock about hard objects by way of assuring himself that they have the metaphysical substantiality he is sure they lack (one thinks of the Berkeley episode): "Johnson is always searching for objects, 'objects adequate to the mind of man,' which are yet not created by that mind, objects, which possess the certainty and stability of an objective existence.

He is always, in effect, striking out at the world, reaffirming its existence and his own, struggling against the ever-present threat of subjectivity, vanity, and vacuity" (390).

Boyd speaks of the infinitude of mind; it is evident from the "Vanity of Human Wishes"—as from *Rasselas* and the *Rambler* and *Idler* essays—that desire aroused a similarly intense fear in Johnson. The infinitude of desire makes the whole world irremediably unsatisfying and, in this sense, insubstantial. But desire is so insistent that, even after learning this lesson, it still circles longingly back toward objects in the world. After the crises that strip them of their power, the characters in the poem mournfully reflect on all that they have lost, as if they had not turned wearily and restlessly from their possessions when they had them. It is as if they were unable to learn the lesson of vanity that the poem was using them to inculcate. But they are not the only ones who fail to learn: the poem's speaker too dwells ruefully on the catalog of the characters' losses after their crises. Though the sense of the stories up to their crises is that desire is vain because of its insatiability, the poet-speaker concludes the stories by evoking the characters' lost grandeur and wealth as if that loss were the crucial lesson. He says of Wolsey: "At once is lost the Pride of aweful State, / The golden Canopy, the glitt'ring Plate, / The regal Palace, the luxurious Board," and so on (113–15). Charles XII dies at a "petty Fortress" by a "dubious Hand," having been condemned to wait "a needy Supplicant"; no "subverted Empire" marked his end (213–20). Similarly, Xerxes takes his flight in a "single Skiff" on an "insulted Sea" (237–38). These tart lines are meant to impress upon us the direness of the catastrophe that overtakes even the greatest power; but the rueful sense of humiliation in them offers the odd consolation that, after all, there are things in the world it is reasonable to desire. It really is too bad to lose the golden canopy, it really would be better not to have to row across the Mediterranean in a skiff.

However dreadful these moments are, at least they do not threaten the characters, or the poet, with the frenzy of insatiable desire that precedes them. Instead, the characters return to a state of feeling—the normal state of wishing for things—whose vanity they, we, and Johnson all presumably discovered by reflecting on their stories. Considering the insanity into which the characters had gone careening, it would appear that this return to a normal state of desire is necessary to mental health. In this sense, no one can learn the lesson about vanity that the poem is inculcating. Even Johnson, the author of the lesson, keeps circling back to a perspective of longing. A famous story about him hints at this. Mrs. Piozzi tells how she found him reading the poem one evening, and how, when he reached the section about the aspiring scholar and the miseries he faces, Johnson burst into tears.[12] Assuming that the lines re-awakened the despair he felt when he was forced to leave Oxford, we would say that he was weeping over lines he had written twenty years before, drawing the moral of a disappointment that had be-fallen him twenty years before *that.* Johnson's desire, like the poem, was always in the present tense.

The circling pattern of the poem's stories suggests that desire is at the heart of experience. After the crisis which each character faces, objects in the world would seem to be simply counters in the char-acter's struggle with desire. Instead of solid objects, they become reassurances, or pieces of evidence; desiring them becomes impor-tant primarily because it allays fear about desire's insatiability; and their substantiality, the difficulty of acquiring them, is an assurance that desire will not exhaust them. Perhaps the same is true even before the crisis comes. Certainly, if these stories are right, the world never offers desire anything it really wants. If we fail to see this, it would seem to be because we are always under a delusion, not because the world is ever what desire craves. "Man has surely some latent sense for which this place affords no gratification," says Ras-selas, "or he has some desires distinct from sense which must be satisfied before he can be happy" (13). Perhaps, then, rather than face the despair of this possibility, desire fixes on the unattainability and resistance of objects by way of lending them a substantiality which, as far as desire is concerned, they do not have. On this view, Johnson's interest in loss could be read the way D. V. Boyd reads his striking out at the world: fearing to lose objects dissimulates the fear that they are insignificant to us.

One object, however, that cannot be construed as this kind of defensive distraction, a mere reassurance that the world will not disintegrate under the ray of desire, is the accumulation of other people's desires. If desire, taken by itself, reduces the whole world to an array of satellites around the central pulse of itself, there is a question about what happens when there are a lot of such central pulses. In the poem this question poses itself in the issue of exemplarity. Given that vanity is universal and that everyone suffers equally from the futility of wishing, then before Johnson can write about this problem, he has to decide which examples deserve attention. After all, there is a real difference between one person's hopeless wishing and another's, and this difference cannot be construed as a mere therapeutic ruse or useful fiction. For Johnson, the world does lack substantiality in the sense that it never satisfies desire; but all the same this does not make the world a phantasm of desire, for any one person's vanity is always just one example among millions of other examples of the same theme. The world has *that* kind of substantiality.

The poem's first story, the paragraph about the statesman, tells how people are singled out. The process is impersonal. However colossal desire is in itself, here it is submerged in the movement of a crowd and made, as it were, to take a number:

> Unnumber'd Suppliants croud Preferment's Gate,
> Athirst for Wealth, and burning to be great;
> Delusive Fortune hears th'incessant Call,
> They mount, they shine, evaporate, and fall. (73–76)

The statesman begins in a crowd of "Unnumber'd Suppliants"; he is ambitious, and so are the rest of them, but ambition only gets him into the process, it does not explain his rise or fall. He rises, as far as one can tell from the ballistic pattern of "they mount, they shine," because of a kind of mechanical pressure: so many suppliants are crowding the gate in hopes of entering the "Frame of Gold" (86) that they have to move in sequence, like molecules in a chamber, in order not to be crushed. Along the way the statesman does indeed enter the frame, becoming a "painted Face" (83), the object of public attention, and in that position his desires, like those of Wolsey or Xerxes, lend themselves readily to reflection in a satirical poem about the vanity of wishes. But they have to be singled out first from an undifferentiated mass, and the force that so distinguishes them is not in his power, but arises from the movement of the crowd.[13] Subsequently, the statesman is swept out of power just as helplessly as he is swept in. His moment of personal distinction is a function, a temporary epiphenomenon, of an impersonal mechanism.

The paragraph stresses that we do not understand this process. Relations of cause and effect are unclear. For instance, Johnson says that people explain the statesman's downfall by pointing to the ugliness of his portrait after it has been cast aside and defaced: "The Form distorted justifies the Fall" (89). The satirical point seems plain: in the venal world of politics, people are loyal only to success, and they rationalize their fickleness with transparent illogic. But Johnson himself does not explain why the statesman falls. This is another place where the crisis in the character's life seems just to happen, as if it were the most obvious thing in the world. The poem says that rising to power brings many dangers, but people do rise; and then we are simply told: "Love ends with Hope, the sinking Statesman's Door / Pours in the Morning Worshiper no more" (79–80). Perhaps the statesman has lost his patron, the poem does not explain; but as the story is framed here, the action takes place entirely between the statesman and his supporters. On this account it sounds circular: the statesman loses his following because he is sinking; but it is as if he were sinking because he was losing his following. We are also told, "For growing Names, the weekly Scribbler lies" (81): the press is attracted to a growing name, but in the absence of any other explanation, one would say that a name grows because it attracts the press. These lines, which mean to depict the statesman's helpless passivity as power slips away from him, reflect his helplessness in the form of bewilderment. The crowd acts unaccountably: suddenly everything is going wrong, and by way of explanation, the observer can only stammer out circular arguments. (He says, in effect, "the crowd likes popular people.")

The circularity conveys a feeling of brute fact, though a fact one does not directly experience. Events in the crowd inexplicably just happen; and commentary deals only with their aftereffects. Thus the passage's rhetoric emphasizes metonymy and personification. The most active characters are inanimate objects: "the sinking Statesman's Door," "the painted Face" (i.e., the painting), "the Form distorted," and the wall in the paragraph's bizarre last line: "And Detestation rids th'indignant Wall" (90). It is as if the crisis in the statesman's career blotted out the human core of the episode and left only this debris of figuration. The view that the "Form distorted justifies the Fall" is in this sense not very different from the poet-speaker's. Both of them reverse the normal relation between cause and effect, and between representation and reality. By satirizing the first view, though, the poet-speaker shows that he knows that such explanations—his own included—of the crowd's movement are merely rhetorical.

Except for the historical exemplars, all of the poem's characters are, like these objects, figures of speech. They exemplify a kind of synecdoche; the singular form of a noun stands for the plural. Here is an example: "For Gold his Sword the hireling Ruffian draws, / For Gold the hireling Judge distorts the Laws" (25–26). Instead of saying that hireling *judges* distort the laws, Johnson speaks of "the hireling *Judge.*" The same is true of the "sinking Statesman," who stands for the crowd of sinking statesmen, and of the ruffian, the enthusiast, the suppliant, the gen'ral fav'rite, the vet'ran, and the teeming mother. Each of the figures has thus a name, but it would be impossible to encounter any of them as one might encounter Wolsey or Charles XII or even figures like "hireling judges" and "ruffians." In this use of synecdoche we are now likely, perhaps, to hear the pomposity and dreariness of a style of moral seriousness which represents what we find most dismal about eighteenth-century literature.[14] But given the context of the poem, the synecdoche also means that when one turns away from the crowd to represent an individual subject, one has to do it by way of a figure of speech. The specificity of the "the" is empty, or figurative; and it has to be empty; for in a crowd it is arbitrary to single out one story rather than another.

At one point, Johnson writes about trying to bring personal experience into contact with the synecdochic use of "the," so that the rhetoric and the narrative would coincide, and one would live out their interaction. This preoccupation lies behind the desire to become famous:

> The festal Blazes, the triumphal Show,
> The ravish'd Standard, and the captive Foe,
> The senate's Thanks, the gazette's pompous Tale,
> With Force resistless o'er the Brave prevail.
> Such Bribes the rapid Greek o'er Asia whirl'd,
> For such the steady Romans shook the World. (175–80)

The use of "the" here denotes that these objects are emblems, that is, not so much immediately given objects as allegorical tokens. But they are all associated, besides, with ritual spectacle and the narrowing and focusing of a crowd's attention onto a single object. In the celebrations around the military hero, the street becomes a theater, and the crowd becomes a community. The "the" is thus not only rhetorical but also literalized. If the image-filled succession of nouns sounds dreamy, like the effusion of someone ("the Brave") steeped in romance literature, that effect only reinforces the passage's wishful ambivalence. Neither the literal nor the figural is primary; instead, they are productively intertwined with each other, as in Wimsatt's mode of the "concrete universal."

In this poem ambition means wanting to become literally "the" one. Otherwise, desire is marginal, not sublimely autonomous. Fame enables desire to act out its tragedy of insatiability. Rhetorically, it promises to elevate the exemplar from the status of an ornamental supplement.

But becoming famous is difficult. It takes "wasted Nations" to "raise a single Name"; and "mortgag'd States their Grandsires Wreaths regret, / From Age to Age in everlasting Debt" (186–88). This difficulty may not be interpreted, like other objects in the poem, as a mere defense against the insatiability of desire. Since overcoming it is a prior condition to one's constitution as an object of representation, since in other words one is no more sublimely autonomous than anyone else until this condition has been met, this difficulty outruns psychological dynamics. It pushes desire aside. Thus it is necessary to give a second account of Johnson's interest in the scattered material, the accumulation of narrative odds and ends, that clutter the poem like detritus. Not only is this jumble something to knock up against to prove to oneself that the world is real; it also displaces the personal; against it, a person's desire is not particularly important.

In the Xerxes passage Johnson provides a figure for this material pressure, a pressure of crowding. After his encountering the Greeks' "rude Resistance," Xerxes reaches his skiff with humbler thoughts, restored to sanity by the world's reassuring flintiness. But the scene's grotesqueness cannot be reduced to a therapeutic fiction:

> The daring Greeks deride the martial Show,
> And heap their Vallies with the Gaudy Foe;
> Th'insulted Sea with humbler Thoughts he gains,
> A single Skiff to speed his Flight remains;
> Th'incumber'd Oar scarce leaves the dreaded Coast
> Through purple Billows and a floating Host. (235–40)

Among "purple Billows and a floating Host" Xerxes' mental rehabilitation cannot be the only thing that counts.

Four

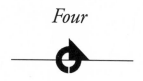

Exemplary Self-Sacrifice

Some of Johnson's moral essays briefly characterize how it feels to be in a crowd. They speak of "evaporation," and "expansion" of the spirits, a dread of "oblivion." These terms are about all he offers; but more can be said, given the role of the crowd in Johnson's skepticism about moral generalization. How does it feel to adopt that skepticism? Moral thought permeates Johnson's conception of human character. Would the skepticism linked here to crowds induce an "evaporation" of character as such? What would that look like?

Critics argue that Johnson's skepticism about generalization expresses and amplifies his preoccupation with the texture of lived experience. His attention to particulars leads naturally to his taste for biography. If one is to convey moral instruction, it will have to be by way of the concrete scenes of real lives with their complexity of circumstance and subtlety of psychological shading. Johnson writes so scrupulously about the texture of the everyday that he belongs, according to one critic, to a realist tradition which extends from Homer to Flaubert (Edinger 91–92).

It is surely true that Johnson writes skeptically about generalization; but is it also true that that skepticism promotes a realist writing style that attends to the texture of the everyday? The theme of crowding, which helps unsettle the effort of generalization, does not necessarily encourage greater interest in personal experience. In many of Johnson's moral essays, as we have seen, it seems rather to highlight its insignificance. How would it feel to live exclusively in public, exposed to crowds? It might well shake one's confidence in generalizing about the nature of human experience, but would it promote a feeling for the "concrete universal" and the deep moral significance of one's day-to-day life?

In *The Life of Savage,* Johnson writes about a character in just this predicament. And though it is a great, evocative biography, to my ear it is not quite a "realist" one. It offers a view of what it is like to live in a crowd; but the picture does not suggest an intensification of the feeling of everydayness. It suggests rather that, where the crowd induces skepticism about moral generalization, one might experience simply that disturbance of certainty and understanding: a merely negative breakdown of one way to make sense of things.

———

Johnson presents Richard Savage's literary career, particularly the phase in which Savage spread the story of his unhappy childhood, as an example of literature's morally improving effects. Savage's early patrons, the ones who were touched by his misfortunes, supported him, Johnson tells us, on principle. The "Inhumanity of his Mother," said Richard Steele about Savage, "had given him a Right to find every good Man his Father."[1] Johnson records how the circulation of the story awakened this sentiment in a range of listeners and readers: in Steele, who helped Savage, Johnson says, "with all the Ardour of Benevolence which constituted his Character" (13); in Robert Wilks, whose "Virtues . . . are not often to be found in the World" (17); and in Mrs. Oldfield, who treated Savage, despite her "sullied" character, with a "Liberality" (19) unmatched by any of his later patrons—including the queen, as Johnson twice points out. The public responded sympathetically, too. When Aaron Hill published an account of the story, Savage found seventy guineas sent to him at a coffeehouse "in Consequence of the Compassion excited by Mr. *Hill's* pathetic Representation" (26). During his imprisonment, another account was published; and the "Compassion of Mankind operated so powerfully in his Favour, that he was enabled, by frequent Presents, not only to support himself, but to assist Mr.

Gregory in Prison" (40). And later, when he wrote the story himself at length in *The Bastard,* his readers at Bath, where his mother was vacationing, spontaneously mounted a public humiliation of her (71). Johnson himself, in the course of telling the story, observes that "[t]his Mother is still alive" (39): he, too, evidently wants to see the story flower into visible moral effects as he tells it.

The story's moral effects come by way of its poignancy. It stirs such pity in listeners that they are compelled to act to relieve Savage's distress. Their acts should in turn affect us by their own poignancy. Johnson is careful to emphasize it: Mr. Wilks, "to whom Calamity seldom complained without Relief," performed his acts of kindness "to the Time of his Death" (18); Mrs. Oldfield, following a "heroic Intention," was "contented with doing good without stipulating for Encomiums" (79); and when telling how Savage himself charitably and compassionately shared his last guinea with a prostitute who had testified against him, Johnson is in his turn moved: "This is an Action which in some Ages would have made a saint, and perhaps in others a Hero," he writes (40). Morality appears thus as a communication of pathos: Savage's story moves his listeners, the story of their benevolence moves us.

By contrast, the great wickedness is Savage's mother's lack of feeling, the lack that made her not simply cruel, but cruel for no reason. She seemed to lack interiority; she presented a blank which Johnson wonders over in tones of horror.[2] She had "proclaimed" the adulterous liaison that had made her pregnant with Savage, and so the dread of shame and of poverty "cannot be supposed" to have "over-balance[d] that natural Affection of a Parent," and made her "look upon her Son from his Birth with a kind of Resentment and Abhorrence" (6). Her announcement to the father that Savage was dead was "perhaps the first Instance of a Lie invented by a Mother to deprive her Son of a Provision which was designed him by another, and which she could not expect herself, though he should lose it" (9).

It is "natural to enquire," Johnson writes later, after recounting that the mother lied in order to suspend the queen's pardon of Savage, "for what Reason she could employ all the Arts of Malice and all the Snares of Calumny, to take away the Life of her own son, of a Son who never injured her, who was never supported by her Expence, nor obstructed any Prospect of Pleasure or Advantage" (38). The essential wickedness was her sheer incalculability, the absence of comprehensible human motives. She was "inhuman," as Steele said, but specifically in the sense that, where others would have reasons and feelings, she offered a blank; and the fact that her crime consisted in reducing Savage to a blank as well, stripping him of name, family, home, class standing, suggests that pity is the key moral act in the *Life* first of all because it betokens emotional life and interiority. Pity filled in the gap produced by the mother's cruelty. It restored or replaced the supports of identity that Savage had lost—giving him a new name, a new father, a new home. And by exercising itself in the form of selfless benevolence, it enacted the traditional promise of martyrdom that losing oneself may be a path to finding oneself. Thus the selfless benevolence of Mrs. Oldfield and Savage was ultimately a noble form of self-aggrandizement: giving what they had without hope of recompense, they recovered themselves as "saints" or "heroes."[3]

But in Savage's hands, this story feels like a spiel or gimmick: like his "gross" dedications to patrons (30) and his perfunctory encomiums upon the queen (79), it offered sentiment for cash. When it produced a lot of cash, Savage was delighted and told the story "in a very uncommon Strain of Humour, and with a Gaiety of Imagination" (27); and when it no longer "procured" him supporters (68), he stopped telling it. The crassness of his milking of the story is a little breathtaking. The empty sentiment of his later poems seems simply debased and depressing; but with the exploitation of the childhood story, which offered a poignant image of self-loss in the figure of the child Savage and which illustrated the redemption of that loss through the action of pity, it was not just a question of faking a sentiment, but of ironizing sentiment itself.

To the theme of the redemption of the self through selfless benevolence, Savage responded by redeeming himself in a different sense: he found in his own marginalization a gimmick he could live off of. At the same time, he seems never to have adopted this ironic attitude as an avowed position. Though he was "not . . . a good Man," he was the "Friend of Goodness" (74); and when he "promote[d] no other Purposes than those of Virtue" (54), Johnson says, he was sincere. He seemed hypocritical and cynical because he cultivated the friendship of people whom he ridiculed (45); but Johnson gives the impression that this inconsistency, the law of his relationships with his patrons, arose, rather, from the faintness of the impression which people made on him, and which rendered his feelings about them not so much contradictory as disconnected. He thought one thing, then another. When he ridiculed Richard Steele, his tirelessly kind patron, this was an example of the "common weakness" which leads almost all people, "sometimes, in the Wantonness of thoughtless Mirth, or the Heat of transient Resentment, [to] speak of their Friends and Benefactors with Levity and Contempt, though in cooler Moments they want neither Sense of their Kindness, nor Reverence for their Virtue" (16). Savage's fault was "rather Negligence than Ingratitude" (16). As a negligent writer, he was as exploitative as a cynical one, but without a cynic's consciousness of the difference between his words and his deeds. He presented, instead, the spectacle of someone unable to get control of that difference, someone who had learned the sound of a certain way of talking—in this case, the rhetoric of eighteenth-century sentimentalism—but took it in as nothing more than that: a way of talking.

Johnson's reaction to Savage in the *Life,* as critics have often observed, is ambivalent—by turns sympathetic and critical, admiring and appalled.[4] What has been little observed is that Johnson's ambivalence also encompasses the literature of moral instruction which Savage both represents and parodies. Two sentences from the end of the *Life* can serve as examples of this ambivalence. On the one hand, Johnson writes: "Those are no proper Judges of his Conduct who have slumber'd away their Time on the Down of Plenty, nor will a wise Man easily presume to say, 'Had I been in *Savage's* Condition, I should have lived, or written, better than *Savage* ' " (140). On the other hand: "This Relation will not be wholly without its Use, . . . if those, who in Confidence of superior Capacities or Attainments disregard the common Maxims of Life, shall be reminded that nothing will supply the Want of Prudence" (140). One is to be reminded of the importance of prudence, but at the same time no wise man will imagine that in Savage's condition he could have acted on that reminder. Reminding isn't enough; not even reminding the "wise" is enough. The sentences point, in other words, to the difference between knowing a rule and acting on it in a particular case, a difference which they imply is not to be mastered by simply inculcating the rule. It isn't that the rule is doubtful. Johnson's language is absolute: "nothing will supply the Want of Prudence." And since it is the "wise" who are at issue, we can assume that they grasp the rule and accept its authority. They grasp it, but they cannot be sure to apply it. Such is the difference between the two operations.[5]

Savage himself was a wise man, on this account. Johnson praises the "Delicacy" of his sentiments (97), the extensiveness of his learning, and his "Sense of the Efficacy of Religion" (54). The difference between the life and his writings (a kind of difference Johnson similarly worries over in *Rambler* No. 14) can be taken to confirm the purity of his sentiments: "his Actions, which were generally precipitate, were often blameable, but his Writings being the Productions of Study, uniformly tended to the Exaltation of the Mind, and the Propagation of Morality and Piety. . . . These Writings may improve Mankind, when his Failings shall be forgotten, and therefore he must be considered upon the whole as a Benefactor to the World" (74–75). But while the writing can be detached from the life and protected from its contamination, it also risks having no practical value: one is struck that these improving works failed to have the desired effect upon their own author. Johnson reflects this concern when he says that Savage's writings "may" improve mankind; a similar worry shadows his speculation about the *Life*'s not being "wholly without its Use." The modesty of the phrase need not be taken as a merely rhetorical gesture. Johnson could readily conceive that his writings might be wholly without use (much of the work of the *Rambler* series is to imagine a scene in which Johnson's moral instruction might take hold—and in what kind of reader). He was convinced of the importance of the lesson he wanted to convey—convinced, in writing the *Life,* that "whoever hears of [Savage's] Faults, will hear of the Miseries which they brought upon him" (75)—but not convinced that conveying the lesson would do any good. For all its gravity, such a lesson, so little able to guarantee itself the accomplishment of its purposes, must inevitably risk feeling, at least to its author, as hollow and parodic as Savage's too-often-repeated sentimental tale. The *Life* thus mulls Savage over as a figure offering some illustrations of how moral instruction can fail to take hold; but Johnson has meanwhile an edgy view to judging how useless his own writing preoccupations might be, and how disastrous (or not) it might be if those preoccupations in fact turned out to be useless.

————

The main reason moral instruction failed to correct Savage's behavior, Johnson writes, was that he was incapable of taking blame. This fault was an elaboration of his sentimentalism. He avoided blaming himself by construing himself as a victim, especially of circumstances beyond his control. By way of example, Johnson observes how Savage consoled himself when the public neglected his work. He complained as he did about his childhood: he saw himself as misunderstood, and "observed how slowly poetical Merit had often forced its Way into the World" (72). Sometimes he blamed the ungovernable logistics of publishing, whose operation he could only watch helplessly: "either [his writings] were published at a Time when the Town was empty, or when the Attention of the Publick was engrossed by some Struggle in the Parliament, or some other Object of general Concern; or they were by the Neglect of the Publisher not diligently dispersed, or by his Avarice not advertised with sufficient Frequency" (73). Savage failed to take the force of moral lessons because of this habit of blaming circumstance. In particular, he never learned from experience. Johnson represents his condition as the misery of a constant motion that took him nowhere:

> By imputing none of his Miseries to himself, he continued to
> act upon the same Principles, and follow the same Path; was

never made wiser by his Sufferings, nor preserved by one Misfortune from falling into another. He proceeded throughout his Life to tread the same Steps on the same Circle; always applauding his past Conduct, or at least forgetting it, to amuse himself with Phantoms of Happiness, which were dancing before him; and willingly turned his Eyes from the Light of Reason, when it would have discovered the Illusion, and shewn him, what he never wished to see, his real State. (74)

This psychic wandering required of Savage a life of physical wandering, for he avoided facing the consequences of his actions by keeping himself continually in flight. He made no lasting friends; he was so unwilling to be held accountable to anyone that his friendships always ended in conflict and bitterness. But Johnson says he was so appealing on first acquaintance that he could form friendships instantaneously, and so was able to live by constantly fleeing, constantly leaping from wreckage to wreckage like the Flying Dutchman:

> [H]is Conversation was so entertaining, and his Address so pleasing, that few thought the Pleasure which they received from him dearly purchased by paying for his Wine. It was his peculiar Happiness, that he scarcely ever found a Stranger, whom he did not leave a Friend; but it must likewise be added, that he had not often a Friend long, without obliging him to become a Stranger. (60)

But he was in constant flight because he had been abandoned and had "been obliged from his first Entrance into the World to subsist upon Expedients" (60). Placing blame is consequently difficult. Originally, Savage's absent mother (we are told) was to blame. But he could have supported her absence if London had provided a substitute for her. The problem with Savage was his "habituation" to living by chance, and this habit he acquired from life in London.

Johnson's account of London stresses the precariousness and impersonality of the relationships between people there. They are precarious because of the power of the city's crowds, which enable unnamed destructive forces to circulate without warning. Rumors got Savage into trouble several times: they destroyed his friendship with Steele, they nearly persuaded the queen to cast him off. But why they circulated at all was a mystery, since, according to Johnson, they served no one's interests. Savage competed several times with a crowd of rivals for the favor of aristocratic patrons; and why he failed where others succeeded was doomed likewise to remain a mystery since, in the crowd, he could never locate the agency by which decisions were made. Johnson keeps the narrative voice at enough of a remove from the events that Savage seems rather to have been involved predominantly with crowds, crowds as such, than with individuals. Friends, rivals, benefactors: all form anonymous crowds in Johnson's telling. The effect is to stress that they just came and went: that "strangers became friends" and that, shortly thereafter, "friends became strangers." None of them leaves any special impression; Johnson never numbers any of *these* streaks of the tulip; and so we see nothing but the pattern. Johnson leaves unnamed the group of patrons under whose power Savage came in his last years, and who dictated his behavior—where he lived, what he wore—with a weird bureaucratic unanswerability. Their anonymity gives their decrees, in Johnson's account, the inevitability, not of royal will, but of a will that cannot be located in any other subject than "they": the "they" of paranoia; or of received ideas, as in "they say that . . ."

In this setting, living by "expedients," as Savage did, feels like a rational strategy for survival. When the next gust of rumor may blow down your patron's support like a house of cards, it's a good thing to be able, like Savage, to keep moving. Perhaps he experienced London as an anonymous crowd because he treated everyone as disposable—surely Johnson's rapid, summary outline of Savage's friendships is meant to indicate how Savage could take or leave them—but the city he came into was already disposing of people that way. Besides, he seems to have built a sense of identity out of his homelessness. Living upon chance was a means of surviving when he had no home; but as the story wears on, it seems increasingly a point of pride with Savage, an antidomestic sensibility that he aggressively cultivated. Johnson repeatedly explains that Savage estranged friends, as he glided from house to house, by rejecting the constraint of homely etiquette. Johnson's language suggests willfulness: Savage spread a "Subversion of all Oeconomy" (98), he seemed "ambitious to overthrow" household order (98), he had the "Practice of prolonging his Visits, to unseasonable Hours, and disconcerting all the Families into which he was admitted" (118), "he continued still to harass, with his nocturnal Intrusions, those that yet countenanced him, and admitted him to their Houses" (119). Johnson gives him the momentum and charisma of a Lord of Misrule: "If he was entertained in a Family, nothing was any longer to be regarded there but Amusements and Jollity; wherever *Savage* entered he immediately expected that Order and Business should fly before him, that all should thenceforward be left to Hazard, and that no dull Principle of domestic Management should be opposed to his Inclination, or intrude upon his Gaiety" (99).

John Dussinger has argued that Savage defended himself against the pain of abandonment by looking for father substitutes;[6] but it seems truer to say that he defended himself, especially after all hope of appealing to the mother broke down, by willfully embracing his condition of homelessness, and priding himself on needing neither a home nor a mother. By the time he received Tyrconnel's patronage and, to that extent, his mother's recognition, he was so accustomed to living upon chance that his old habits persisted even though he no longer had any contingencies to defend himself against. If this might be seen as the moment of excess, the moment when Savage was to blame for the misery that followed,[7] it might also be taken as a sign of how much his disavowal of obligation and authority was a matter of psychological survival.

Reading the moral lesson of Savage's experience is hard, though, not only because his failings may have been necessary to his survival. In talking about crowds, it is also hard, maybe impossible, to grasp the relation between individuals and circumstances. In a crowd it is unclear how to attribute consequences to someone's actions; it can be unclear whether one's actions have any effect at all.

In personal relationships, seeing consequences is an everyday necessity; but Savage, the Savage in the *Life,* seems to live among crowds, not among persons, and what he is responsible for in his dealings with them is far from clear. Johnson points to this problem when he illustrates Savage's moral irresponsibility: as his key example, he describes Savage's rationalizations about his publishing disappointments, that is, his disappointments as a writer addressing an anonymous crowd. Savage failed to learn from experience; specifically, he failed to blame himself when the public declined to read his writing. In blaming the vagaries and accidents of publishing he was plainly looking, as Johnson suggests, for an excuse to avoid self-examination. A reader faithful to the obligation to attend to a story's moral would have deciphered in Savage's publishing experiences some message about his failings. But it is not certain that one can read a personal message in the movements of public opinion. The vanity of that kind of reading is the point of the *Rambler* essay (No. 146) in which Johnson describes how an author whose new pamphlet has been neglected by the public jumps desperately to the conclusion that his "enemies" have sabotaged his publication. According to this *Rambler,* an author will fantasize any personal relation with the public, even a hostile relation, rather than acknowledge an impersonal one. For in an impersonal relation, the notions that tell us who we are—in particular, notions of praise and blame—count for nothing. From this perspective, one would be entitled to say that Savage recognized an important truth about his publishing ventures. It would be self-deceiving to expect, like the protagonist of *Rambler* No. 146, that one would have a chance here to renounce vanity and self, and, when it was appropriate, to take the blame. If it feels all the same that Johnson is right about Savage, that would just force one to radicalize one's sense of how strange publishing is: it's so strange that either imagining of an author's relation to it is a mystification—the relation of passive victim which Savage counted on, as well as that of moving force satirized in the *Rambler* essay.

A different kind of publication and a different kind of crowd appear in the central scene of lesson-learning, the scene in which Savage's writing manages to punish his mother. This crowd has something like a ritual purpose; the scene is like a holiday festival. Johnson writes that when Savage published *The Bastard,* a poem attacking his mother, she was at Bath, "where she could not conveniently retire from Censure, or conceal herself from Observation; and no sooner did the Reputation of the Poem begin to spread, than she heard it repeated in all Places of Concourse, nor could she enter the Assembly Rooms, or cross the Walks, without being saluted with some Lines from *The Bastard"* (71). As in other passages where writing edifies—for example, where Hill's preface brings in seventy pounds for Savage at the coffeehouse, or where Johnson writes that "this mother is still alive," as if inviting us to do something about her—the scene at Bath represents a bridging of the gap between the public and the private. The author here can use his publication to address immediate personal concerns in the manner of an advice column or a telethon. Because of its immediacy, this sort of writing can have readily identifiable practical effects. It is useful writing. Johnson makes out the scene at Bath as more than a humiliation: it is a punishment and also an education, the scene where Savage's mother learns her lesson. He says that this "was perhaps the first Time that she ever discovered a Sense of Shame" (71–72). It was the first time she was confronted with, or more importantly, unable to ignore, what she had done. She was "unable," Johnson reports contentedly, savoring the moment where the effects of literary edification were so clear, "to bear the Representation of her own Conduct" (72). The crowd nailed her down to this, stopped the evasions of suppression and rationalization. Johnson says in *Rambler* No. 155 that one doesn't need to learn from others what one's faults are—one always knows what they are already (5:60). But others confer identity in a different sense: they take it out of one's power to repress and reinterpret it (5:61). The crowd at Bath, a crowd to which one could have a personal relation, was in this sense one place where interpretation could come to the end of the line.

Such, at any rate, would be the elusive hope behind the scene, the hope suggested by Johnson's tone of complacent approval, and the "great satisfaction" he says that Savage expressed when he "used to relate" this story (apparently he told it often) (71). But it is an elusive hope. Though it marks the conclusion of Savage's dealings with his mother and the culmination of the *Life*'s moral exposure of her, the scene has virtually no impact either on the relationships between any of the characters or on the shape and movement of the story. Instead of a tragedy's high point, it reads as a mere anecdote. The setting is suggestive. Bath was traditionally a sacred spot; kings had been crowned there, and the diseased and crippled hoped for miraculous cures from the waters of its hot spring. But in the sixteenth century, it became a vacation resort, and in the eighteenth century it was transformed into an aristocratic pleasure garden, though one which still retained some of its old reputation as a pilgrimage site.[8] It continued as separate from the commerce of ordinary life as before, but now it was unclear whether it was more meaningful than other places or less so. In such a setting, the punishment of Savage's mother feels ambiguous. It can't help seeming as idle as a (vicious) vacation resort entertainment, though it also resembles the grave violence of a moral code's ritual enactment. It is as fragile and transient as a phantom—a relic of a system of moral policing it seems as much to travesty as harken back to. At any rate the scene had no lasting effect. Johnson points out that Savage's mother did not remain long at Bath. "She fled from Reproach, though she felt no Pain from Guilt, and left *Bath* with the utmost Haste, to shelter herself among the Crowds of *London*" (72).

In other biographies Savage appears a much less lonely and persecuted figure than he does in the *Life*. Though Johnson mentions numerous friends and patrons by name, he only sketches them in outline; they leave a faint impression. He does not describe the day-to-day course of these friendships, so they do not seem lived and ongoing. Nor does he observe that they formed an extended web. When he mentions Aaron Hill, the publisher of the *Plain-Dealer* who presented Savage's case in his magazine in the mid-1720s, he does not speak of Hill's circle of protégés and friends, who wrote poems and novels about one another, and two of whom—Eliza Haywood and Martha Sansom—had affairs with Savage.[9] Johnson refers twice to Thomson and once to Mallet, but gives no indication that they exchanged poems with Savage and in this way communally worked up a new poetic style (Holmes 83–87). Savage lived in a community: that is, he saw and judged and was himself likewise judged and seen. But the *Life* creates an eerie effect of isolation, as if he were a sheer spectacle or conversely an invisible spectator. At most, he appears as someone to be coaxed and managed; only once or twice (and very briefly) as a partner or a friend.

Critics agree that Johnson projected hopes and fears onto Savage; the *Life*'s effect of spooky isolation is evidently one of these. Richard Holmes observes that Savage himself had formed a rhetoric and image of the poet as a social outcast, especially in his fantasmagorical and paranoid poem *The Wanderer* from the late 1720s; and when Johnson came to London in 1737, he was disposed in many respects to embrace that rhetoric and image (40–41). He was poor, he was new to the city, he was unhappily married, he was disappointed in his academic prospects, and he was desperate for work as a writer. When he fell under Savage's spell, as people readily did, he did so, it appears, partly on the grounds of their shared social disaffection. The stories of their nighttime wanderings through the streets refer to their denunciations of the government; and the poem "London" and the pamphlet on the "Norfolk Stone" both reflect Savage's political and social anger. It seems reasonable to assume, then, that Johnson used the *Life* to meditate on Savage as an example of how to bear and even simply to conceptualize the condition of severe social estrangement in the city. He was trying to find out what to do and what not to do; and he was seeing sometimes what he wanted and working to look clearly at what he dreaded.

He is absorbed particularly by the marvel of Savage's indomitable cheerfulness; he recurs to it with an insatiable interest (99, 102, 104, 109, 120, 125, 126). But the first time he speaks of it, he seems to condemn it on moral grounds. He speculates that "it would be perhaps of some Benefit . . . if the Practice of Savage could be taught" (73–74), that is, the practice of shifting the blame; but he then rejects the idea because of the failure to learn, the moral obtuseness, that it entails (74). It was Savage's failure to assume responsibility for the troubles in his life, his inability to learn from experience, that kept him in high spirits no matter how desperate his circumstances became.

Johnson's persistence in celebrating a cheerfulness with so shaky a moral foundation suggests that the moral objection does not settle the issue for him. Why might it not? He says that Savage's practice would perhaps be of benefit "if adventitious and foreign Pleasures must be persued" (73). He means specifically the pleasures of fame and publishing. They are inherently illusory and unstable; he opposes them to what is "doubtless to be wished": "that Truth and Reason were universally prevalent; that every thing were esteemed according to its real Value; and that Men would secure themselves from being disappointed in their Endeavours after Happiness, by placing it only in Virtue, which is always to be obtained" (73). In the world of publishing, truth and reason are not universally prevalent, it is hard to establish anything's real value, and applause has no clear relation to virtue. To write and publish is a kind of folly by which one submits one's happiness to the lawless vicissitudes, the "adventitious and foreign" authority, of public opinion. As a consolation, Savage's practice is only a less unhappy alternative among a choice of evils; Johnson recommends it diffidently, with the hope "that Folly might be an Antidote to Folly, and one Fallacy be obviated by another" (74). But the moral objection to Savage has no hold here. With authors, "adventitious and foreign Pleasures must be persued," and so Savage's cheerfulness will continue to look inviting even after its moral irresponsibility has been laid bare. Johnson is interested in it, I think, because as a penniless author in London, he too finds himself in circumstances where the rhetoric of virtue is not enough. It is one of the *Life's* grim aspects, though, that Savage's cheerfulness appears not enough either.

Savage kept up his morale by seeing himself as a victim of circumstance, but he also imagined that he was his own master. He asked for favors "without the least Submission or apparent Consciousness of Dependence" (98). When he received stipends from Tyrconnel and from his anonymous benefactors, he haughtily antagonized them as if he owed them nothing. He did not "use the Advantages he enjoyed with that Moderation which ought to have been with more than usual Caution preserved by him, who knew, if he had reflected, that he was only a Dependent on the Bounty of another" (66). In a passage about the defiant letter Savage wrote his benefactors from prison, Johnson deplores Savage's ludicrous self-indulgence: "Such was his Imprudence, and such his obstinate Adherence to his own Resolutions, however absurd. A Prisoner! supported by Charity!" (132).

To be able to assert his independence so angrily, even as he was depending for a living on others and blaming circumstances for his misfortunes, Savage had to believe in some notion of self or character beyond circumstance, a sheet-anchor of psychic integrity around which material and moral concerns like borrowing from a friend or losing a patron might toss about insignificantly. He had, in Fredric Bogel's words, "a willingness to act and to judge as though he were accountable only to himself."[10] Bogel quotes a letter in which Savage explained why he had added "delineated" to the title of his poem on London and Bristol:

> Why did Mr *Woolaston* add the same Word to his Religion of Nature? I suppose that it was his Will and Pleasure to add it in his Case; and it is mine to do so in my Own. You are pleased to tell me, that you understand not, why Secrecy is injoin'd, and yet I intend to set my Name to it [the poem on London and Bristol]. My Answer is—I have my private Reasons; which I am not obliged to explain to any One. (131–32)

The chaos of his life, which made it hard to see how to bring principles to bear on events, might have made him doubt whether he counted for anything, but instead it convinced him of—or drove him, perhaps, desperately to insist on—his transcendent importance. The testiness of the commentary on Savage's illusion of independence suggests that this notion of self is the main source of Johnson's dissatisfaction with Savage's cheerfulness. He is attracted to Savage, I think, because he envies his cheerfulness—specifically the cheerfulness that survived the city's impersonality, borne in upon him by poverty, homelessness, sleeping in the streets, the transitoriness of friendships, and the inscrutability of public opinion; but he is ambivalent about Savage to the extent that his cheerfulness was founded on a belief in the self's autonomy.

The notion of an autonomous self independent of moral judgment is in conflict with Johnson's conviction of our fundamentally social nature and our dependency on one another, a conviction which shapes his whole manner of representing character. His conception of biographical portraiture is predominantly didactic. He seeks not so much to show a character as to illustrate larger moral ideas with it. In *Rambler* No. 60, he praises biography because, more than any other literary form, it persuasively "diffuse[s] instruction to every diversity of condition" (3:319). Moral ideas often lose their hold on the mind because of their generality; they fail "for want of particular reference, and immediate application" (R 87, 4:94). Biography brings them to life through attention to the "minute details of daily life" (3:321).[11] These invite readers to find in biography parallels to their own lives; and by appealing thus to readers' self-regard, they "enchain the heart" (3:319). Johnson is accordingly anxious to gather as many telling details of a life as he can; but though such details form a vivid psychological portrait, Johnson's rhetoric is not predominantly psychological but didactic;[12] and one seems to read not just about a character but about an array of moral ideas which go to make up a character.[13]

The Life of Savage, for example, which draws a vivid and detailed picture, is nevertheless thoroughly permeated with the rhetoric of moral instruction, so much so that here the notion of a nonmoral character, a character one would understand just in itself, seems a virtual contradiction in terms: it is through the vocabulary of moral reflection that we understand character.[14] The *Life* is like a collection of fables. It has a fable's rhythm of episode and moral commentary: Savage's assistance of a prostitute exemplifies "Charity" (40); his letter from prison, "Imprudence" (132), the reckless sale of the rights to his poem, "Slavery to his Passions" (58). Times and places are identified by their moral character ("this was the Golden Part of Savage's Life" [44]; "he was now again abandoned to Fortune" [17]; "he passed the Night sometimes in mean Houses" [97]). Chronological time features rarely and inessentially. At one point, after telling how Savage's first play failed, Johnson says that Savage "wrote two Years afterward" *Love in a Veil* (13). One might wonder what he did in the intervening two years, but the question would be beside the point, just as it would make no sense to wonder what the grasshopper was living on the winter before he met the ant. Similarly, faces and bodies are almost nonexistent in the *Life*. The only description of a person is given in the "character," where Johnson singles out the virtual qualities of Savage's appearance—his "melancholy Aspect," "grave and manly Deportment," and "solemn Dignity of Mien" (135). He also says that Savage was "of a thin Habit of Body," an odd eighteenth-century phrase which makes it sound as if a body could be worn like a suit of clothes (135). Personifications, not persons, predominate in the *Life*. We hear how "Justice and Compassion procured [Savage] an Advocate" (38) and how he looked in high society for "Abilities really exalted above the common Level, or Virtues refined from Passion" (64). His friends and enemies embody moral abstractions: Mr. Wilks was "humane, generous, and candid" (17), Mr. Hill acted with "Humanity and Politeness" (23), Savage's mother showed "implacable and restless Cruelty" (6). These figures combine to form moral tableaux which revolve around Savage like the seasons or like scene changes in the theater. There is the "Golden Part" ("He was courted by all . . . and caressed by all" [44]) and there are the periods of "Merit in Distress" (26): "On a Bulk, in a Cellar, or in a Glass-house among Thieves and Beggars, was to be found the Author of *The Wanderer*, the Man of exalted Sentiments, extensive Views, and curious Observations" (97).

Savage's self-absorption evaded the authority of such didactic language. It did not set him avowedly in opposition to it but induced the "negligence" which, by disjoining his words from his actions, gave him an air of cynicism and slyness, and made him, though a "Friend to Goodness," "not a good Man." Unable to learn the lessons of his own experience, he turned it so practically to account that it began to feel, for all its pathos, like a parody; and having figured as the victim in his tale, he emerged from it—for a while—both rich and unmoved. His spieling relation to the language of edification gave him a kind of wit and glamour. By a certain sneakiness he insinuated himself into places where he seemed not to belong; and in doing so, he seemed charismatically to escape the rules that applied to others, and to justify his attitude of self-sufficiency. His patter kept him from having to work or to meet obligations, and the tale about his mother won him a place in the highest circles of society. His assumption of the title "volunteer laureat," which began his longest literary undertaking, was virtually an open declaration of defiance of the court's system of awards and designations of merit. Colley Cibber, the official laureate, decried Savage's assumption of this title as the theft of a "Mark of Honour" which only the king could bestow (79). Savage, having "stolen" the mark, defended his right to it by claiming that it had no value: "*Savage* did not think any Title, which was conferred upon Mr. *Cibber,* so honourable as that the Usurpation of it could be imputed to him as an Instance of very exorbitant Vanity" (79). As in the use of his childhood story, though more explicitly and deliberately, he proceeded here by making a mockery of the literary position he aimed at, and then got from it what he could; and in the process, he managed to be witty and provocative. It was his way of borrowing without incurring debt.

But once he had gotten his position, he was stuck writing deadly panegyrics to the queen year after year. Having thought to boost himself by exploiting the emptiness of public marks of honor and of court ritual, he found himself chained to that empty language and watching it grow emptier and emptier. This is the central pattern of his story: wily evasion always turns out to be a trap; and mercenary exploitation of traditional tropes and topics in writing leads to literary sterility. For Johnson the prospect of decaying language is a recurrent source of anxiety and despair. The stock of moral topics may or may not already be exhausted (cf. R 2, R 54, A 95), but it is in any case limited; and the moralist is doomed to repeat tired platitudes as freshly as he can: the "imitator treads a beaten walk, and with all his diligence can only hope to find a few flowers or branches untouched by his predecessor, the refuse of contempt, or the omissions of negligence" (R 86, 4:88).[15] Johnson accordingly writes about the tedium of Savage's writing project both with tight-lipped horror and with a sense that it was the inevitable punishment for attempting to exploit for advancement the emptiness of his language:

> He did not appear to consider these Encomiums as Tests of his Abilities, or as any Thing more than annual Hints to the Queen of her Promise, or Acts of Ceremony, by the Performance of which he was intitled to his Pension. . . . Of some of them he had himself so low an Opinion, that he intended to omit them in the Collection of Poems, for which he printed Proposals, and solicited Subscriptions; nor can it seem strange, that, being confined to the same Subject, he should be at some Times indolent, and at others unsuccessful; that he should sometimes delay a disagreeable Task, till it was too late to perform it well; or that he should sometimes repeat the same Sentiment on the same Occasion, or at others be misled by an Attempt after Novelty to forced Conceptions and far-fetched Images. (80)

These passages reflect the *Life's* prevailing dread of senseless repetitive labor and waning energy. Like Savage's fate of "treading the same Steps on the same Circle," to which his failure to read his experience condemned him, this labor befell him as a bad literary experience. One way or another, meaning was always decaying around him. He began his career by writing an elegy for the king. Johnson says that only an ulterior motive could have driven Savage to till so barren a soil: "it must certainly have been with farther Views that he prevailed upon himself to attempt a Species of Writing, of which all the Topics had been long before exhausted, and which was made at once difficult by the Multitudes that failed in it, and those that had succeeded" (30). A time came when his childhood story, through repetition, had likewise gone flat ("His Story, though in Reality not less melancholy, was less affecting, because it was no longer new; it therefore procured him no new Friends" [68]); and when he was stranded in Bristol and nearing starvation, he tried to get back to London by writing a second version of his failed tragedy about Sir Thomas Overbury.

These were his main writing projects. The *Life* notes as well writing projects that seemed to reverse the progress of exhaustion. Johnson praises *On Publick Works* for finding a topic that had never been thought "worthy of the Ornaments of Verse" (92): the colonization of uninhabited territory. And he praises Savage's elegy on the queen for ingeniously linking the topic of her death with her birthday, again a maneuver that revitalizes the genre by introducing a new "topic": "he has formed a happy Combination of Topics, which any other Man would have thought it very difficult to connect in one View, but . . . it may justly be said, that what no other Man would have thought on, it now appears scarcely possible for any Man to miss" (107). Johnson is perhaps being ironic. Donald Greene has argued that Johnson, an anticolonialist, deprecated the scheme of colonizing uninhabited territory as an attempt to solve political problems the way Savage tried to solve his personal ones: by running away.[16] And it is hard to believe that Johnson seriously imagines that Savage was the first elegist to link the topics of birth and death. If the passages are ironic, they reinforce the general impression that Savage's writing career was constantly declining, its energy was waning, and that his attempts to triumph in it or to revitalize it were desperate and deluded.

The pattern of literary exhaustion in the *Life* complements a pattern of material and financial decline—a progressive loss of energy and cessation of movement on the way from London to the Bristol jail—that seems, like his literary decline, the inevitable outcome of treading the same steps on the same circle. If a man stays alive by fleeing, he is naturally apt to meet his end by running out of places to flee to.

Savage not only lost his money and his writerly energy, though. The fablelike style of the *Life* pressures one to sense a form of decline that cannot be identified in these empirical terms. It is as if the man himself became depleted. John Dussinger points it out in his discussion of Savage's clothes. He argues that Johnson details the state of the clothes—from the "fine coat" Justice Page rails against, to the "decayed" rags of Savage's last years—as if the clothes and the life were meant to blur together: "his whole life . . . turns out finally to depend on a 'decent' coat . . . and the 'decay' of his clothes is only an outward sign of 'wearing out his life in expectation.' "[17] Clothes can represent the condition of a "life," and a life can "wear out" like clothes, but only figuratively. The analogy between them supposes a style of characterization that allows for nonrealistic effects. Presumably it is because Johnson makes extensive use of personifications and exemplary tableaux that Savage's life can seem, in this way, thing-like. The portrait's relentless spareness helps foreground the theme of attrition. By paring down what it means to be a character, the *Life* makes the characters peculiarly available to assimilation by material metaphors. Savage seems, for example, to have no intellectual or romantic life; friends and ideas are there only to be accumulated and squandered. (After reading Johnson, it is startling to discover, for example, that Savage had love affairs.)

A life "wears out" like a coat; how does it do that? This is a question about Johnson's metaphorical conceptualization of Savage, his instinct about what went wrong with him. Sometimes Johnson stops the story briefly to recount oddities that seem to catch Savage's character in a single stroke. They serve as exemplary illustrations or emblems intended to illuminate the life's sense in a flash; this is an effect that eighteenth-century biographers, including Johnson, like to juxtapose to their more explicitly elaborated didactic passages. There are at least two such passages in the *Life*—the tailor episode and the paragraph about proofreading—each of which Johnson marks out by explaining that he means in them to show Savage's "character" or his "peculiarity," what it was that drove him.[18] (Two stories about Richard Steele serve the same purpose and have much the same moral.) The passages illustrate Savage's fiercely defensive self-absorption and the decline that follows upon it; but because of their exemplarity, they seem to concern not just the decay of his writing but also the life's general condition. As such, they suggest as well a metaphorical connection between the two themes. That is, a life might "wear out" in the manner of a didactic text—Savage's childhood story, for example—whose structure of exemplarity was breaking down into component topics and illustrations: platitudes (and sentimental clichés) and anecdotes repeated to no purpose. This metaphor seems ready-to-hand for Johnson, given how instinctively he thinks of character as an illustration of general moral concepts and "topics." A character like Savage's, that defines itself in proud independence of received social codes, appears from such a perspective, aside from empirical considerations, as a rhetorical problem, a misfire in the circuit of exemplification.

Both the passages describing Savage's "peculiarity" are about untoward and ill-judged self-assertion. In one of the passages, Johnson explains that Savage's benefactors, in preparation for his forced exile from London, arranged, without asking him first, for a tailor to come to his room. Savage was beside himself with rage. It was atrocious, he told his friends later, that his benefactors "had sent for a Taylor to measure him" (112). Here he was plainly staging a symbolic rebellion against his benefactors when he could not break free from them in actuality. The other passage is more mysterious. It describes Savage's obsessive style of proofreading: how he fretfully revised his punctuation, and how he lamented printer's errors as a "heavy Calamity." He seems to have felt that his personal integrity was in some way at risk in the print shop. Bogel speculates that Savage was demarcating what was his and what was not, due to a fear that his identity was permeable.[19] He had an obsessive "investment in controlling every detail of the mode in which he was to present himself to the world" (196). He was unconcerned about the substance of what he said; but he was fanatically anxious about asserting his rights of authorship (196). Since he wrote most of his poems for patrons he despised, his anxiety about the permeability of his identity is understandable; and it seems a reasonable guess that the fanaticism with which he rooted out printer's errors was a way of lashing out at his patrons, especially if he was as obsessive about the proofs of the poems he hated as he was about those of the poems he cared for. Just as the tailor's measure symbolized his benefactors' power over him, so the forms of typography—and of punctuation, which Johnson says Savage also fretted over incessantly and insatiably—represented the coercion by which his patrons exploited his poetic gift. For the point seems only partly to have been to protect his poetry from mutilation or the printer's encroachment; it was also apparently to stall the poem's publication.

The passages sum up Savage's general resistance to the pressure to comply with established codes of self-display. In his writing, that resistance appeared as a pattern of "negligence" about the moral sentiments he espoused; in these passages, it is suggested metaphorically and schematically in his odd choice of a tailor and a print shop as targets for his frustration. Measuring tape and punctuation marks are similar in that they regulate how we represent ourselves. By rebelling against them, Savage, who was now painfully conscious of his dependency, desperately asserted his deep specialness, a specialness that confounded ordinary forms of representation. He refused to be considered an example of a rule. When he complains that "they had sent for a Taylor to measure him," the scene suggests his resistance to measure in general: he hated the idea that they were measuring not just his body but "him."

Clothing is generally an anxious topic in the *Life*. As Dussinger notices, Savage's decline parallels the decay of his clothes.[20] For a genius especially it appears humiliating to have to depend on good clothes. Savage complained bitterly that people judged his talent by his tailoring: he complained "that as his Affairs grew desperate he found his Reputation for Capacity visibly decline, that his Opinion in Questions of Criticism was no longer regarded when his Coat was out of Fashion" (101). Johnson suggests that Savage's genius was like a body needing to be clothed. The clothing was Tyrconnel's money: "To admire Mr. *Savage* [in his 'Golden Time'] was a Proof of Discernment; and to be acquainted with him was a Title to poetical Reputation. His Presence was sufficient to make any Place of public Entertainment popular; and his Approbation and Example constituted the Fashion. So powerful is Genius, when it is invested with the Glitter of Affluence" (44). Genius arbitrates literary disputes, but it assumes authority only when clothed ("invested") in money, as if it were a body which only properly became a body when dressed. Once the garment wears out, genius, as Savage complained, loses its power. Johnson explains this dependency as a matter of interpretative ease. Money is simple to figure out, wisdom is hard: "As many more can discover, that a Man is richer than that he is wiser than themselves, Superiority of Understanding is not so readily acknowledged as that of Condition" (100). Calculating and comparing sums of money is simple in the sense that, if you can do one calculation, you can do them all; particular sums are just examples of the general rules. But if genius and wisdom have to dress themselves in money in order to be understood and acknowledged, they are in danger of seeming mere examples too. In his "peculiar" moments Savage rebelled against *this* threat. By refusing to be measured and by fretting about the mechanics of proofreading, he repelled the elements of his self-presentation which most obviously followed a code and most readily illustrated the reduction of expression to mere exemplification.

The point of the tailor story is that Savage seems laughable and poignant, but by no means sublimely autonomous, when he insists thus on his dignity and independence. The proofreading story formulates the idea more precisely. Johnson writes: "In one of his Letters relating to an Impression of some Verses, he remarks, that he had with Regard to the Correction of the Proof *a Spell upon him,* and indeed the Anxiety, with which he dwelt upon the minutest and most trifling Niceties, deserved no other Name than that of Fascination" (58; Johnson's italics). He had a "spell upon him." But just at this moment, as with the tailor, he was affirming the singularity, dignity, and freedom of his character, which no expressive form could reflect or define. He was protecting it against the threat of letters, punctuation marks, the printing press:

> A superstitious Regard to the Correction of his Sheets was one of Mr. *Savage's* Peculiarities: he often altered, revised, recurred to his first Reading of Punctuation, and again adopted the Alteration; he was dubious and irresolute without End, as on a Question of the last Importance, and at last was seldom satisfied; the Intrusion or Omission of a Comma was sufficient to discompose him, and he would lament an Error of a single Letter as a heavy Calamity. (58)

Johnson describes as well Savage's habit, especially when he wanted to show his independence, of physically mangling his printed works. When he quarreled with Tyrconnel, and again when he decided he hated his tragedy and his Bangorian poem, he acted out his wrath by destroying old editions, blotting out names, and snatching copies from friends' hands (12, 24, 62). Evidently he hoped to affirm the incommensurability of his character to all these forms; but in doing so he drifted into this frenzy, irresolution, and discomposure. As an exemplary scene, the proofreading passage suggests that this is what being a "character" was like: self-affirmation was like a "spell." When he felt that no punctuation seemed adequate to measure his phrases, that feeling was his way of not knowing what he was saying; insisting that nothing could control him was his way of being helpless; he found himself performing an uncontrolled utterance, but it was like a hypnotic chant, a "spell," possibly a senseless one—at any rate, senseless to him—like speaking in tongues.

In other words, when Savage displayed his character as it was in itself, rather than as illustration of something else, it came out as a blot.[21] Walter Benjamin observes that the individuals in Poe's London crowds seem to be jerky and disconnected in their movements, somewhat as if they were disintegrating: they become an assemblage of what Johnson would call "peculiarities."[22] Some such degradation befell Savage's character, too. He lived wholly among crowds, and consoled himself in the midst of their confusion with the thought that, no matter what, he always had himself; but in its radical individuality beyond moral illustrativeness, his character degenerated into the "adventitious peculiarities" and "superficial dies" of rhetorical failure. It wasn't a rich content that broke down all forms; it exhausted itself in simple refusal. A few hints of drunkenness and moral transgression vaguely link Savage with Dionysian intransigency, "character" with an ungovernable overflow of carnivalesque vitality. But mainly the portrait of Savage's transgressiveness is abstract and devoid of sensuality. Johnson keeps him scrupulously asexual. He says nothing of gambling. Savage killed a man in a tavern brawl; but Dussinger is right that, in Johnson's telling, the scene offers none of the "Bacchanalian release of Fielding's mock battles."[23] If Savage was a Lord of Misrule, he was a skinny one.[24] His peculiarity of character was merely negative, a defiance of lan-

guage that was just erasure. At most it could be displayed with a
joke, like his wisecrack about Cibber.

Johnson remains fascinated by Savage's cheerfulness all the same.
He criticizes Savage's self-deception, but that only means that Savage, who played at being a sentimental hero, drew his cheerfulness
from a misguided notion of his condition; it doesn't prove that such
a condition must necessarily be miserable. Perhaps the language of
"exhaustion" inflects the question in too gloomy a direction. "Exhaustion," as the *Life* talks about it, is itself a topic: Dussinger finds
its antecedent in Boethius's wheel of fortune. On this reading the
Tyrconnel period represented the high point, and on either side
Savage rose and fell. But we might read "exhaustion," instead, as a
kind of entropy: a "fall" into the absence of a pattern. What was the
high point, what was the low one in Savage's life? He was always
poor, and even when he lived with Tyrconnel, he went to pawn-
brokers to supply his expenses and "lamented the Misery of living at
the Tables of other Men" (52) (just as he did when he was sleeping
on the street). He was always scrambling between expedients; some
worked, others didn't. Savage might be seen, then, not as falling (or
growing exhausted) but as enduring an existence without a pattern,
a condition reflected in the *Life*'s distinctive double effect of drive
and inconclusiveness, of hurtling toward an inevitable conclusion
and of piling episodes on one another randomly, first-come first-
served. Savage's decline is palpable, but partly the decline consists in
not being able to draw its moral design. On his deathbed, Savage
did not work out the sense of his life as both the virtuous and the
vicious usually do in eighteenth-century literature. Death closed
nothing off for him, provided no sense of definition; by chance or
by some fatality, his death confirmed (or imitated) the pattern of his
"peculiarity," and he died forgetting what he was going to say.
Disappointingly, he was not cheerful. He informed his keeper that
he had something to tell him; "but after a Pause, moved his Hand in
a melancholy Manner, and finding himself unable to recollect what
he was going to communicate, said '*Tis gone*" (135). Being cheerful
as a character would mean, among other things, cheerfully accepting *that*.

———

Accepting one's littleness is a trait that Johnson wants to praise as a virtue, an important and necessary virtue in the midst of crowds. Savage went wrong in that, in effect, he tried to praise that virtue in himself: he hoped to make himself great by playing the victim. The *Life* exposes the hollowness of the rhetoric that came out of that effort. We see that he was not really resigned to his marginality; that he expected to find a reward of self-esteem in bearing it. But if his resignation were genuine, and someone else were to praise it accordingly, it is not clear that the rhetoric would be less hollow. "On the Death of Dr. Levet" suggests this possibility. Like Savage, Levet "walked his narrow round"; he too was rootless and itinerant. But he was free of Savage's egotism and self-absorption; he had no fancy that he was exempt from social duties or that he was secretly remarkable, like a king in disguise. Johnson pays tribute in his poem to Levet's talent for graceful self-effacement; but he struggles with a feeling that this praise, by virtue of its very publicity, belies its moral lesson.

The poem is arranged as a reminiscence or a sort of flashback. First Johnson invites the reader to see Levet descending to the grave, and then, observing that Levet still "fills affection's eye," he goes on to remember a sequence of scenes, almost like blackouts, that convey a sense of his generosity and reliability. Levet emerges in this way as a figure the poet sees, but who, like a figure in a movie, neither sees nor knows he is being seen. What he is doing is vivid and close to the poet, but at the same time it has the weightlessness and remoteness of a projected image. Johnson describes him entirely from the outside. He is seen as a "vig'rous remedy" administered to "fainting nature" at the point of death; then as the "useful care" present in the hovels of people dying in "hopeless anguish," loneliness, and poverty. Johnson calls him "he" only once—when he is identified as the image that "fills affection's eye." Otherwise he disappears into the visibility of the things associated with him. In two stanzas the grammatical construction implicitly points to him as the subject, so that the absence of the "he" is particularly striking, and creates the effect of his life being rapt away, leaving behind

nothing but images of his presence, external manifestations that
have lost their inner foundation and become hollow surfaces.

> And sure th'Eternal Master found
>   The single talent well employ'd.
>
> The busy day, the peaceful night,
>   Unfelt, uncounted, glided by . . .

The point here is not to deny that there is a powerful connection
between Levet's inner life and his outward actions—for Johnson's
language clearly insists that there is one; but because the "he" is
absent, the description of the connection between inside and outside, despite its effect of intimacy, seems less to bring Levet close to
the reader (and to the poet) than to present his gestures as pure
images—images completely independent of his living presence—
and thus to highlight their irreducible remoteness. There is a moving sense of warmth—a kind of luminous glow—in the poem; but it
is the warmth and glow of a scene in a film or a magic lantern show.

Filling the eye substitutes here for and supervenes on the act of
filling space, which is considered Levet's essential quality. Johnson
sees Levet; but he is saying that before this, the latter was known by
the pressure of his felt presence. His "care was ever nigh," his daily
toil supplied daily wants, his virtues walked a narrow round, "Nor
made a pause, nor left a void." Not only was his own life uninter-
rupted by discontinuities—even time "glided by" for him, "un-
counted," unarticulated by divisions—but also he filled the gaps in
other people's lives. The importance of his influence as this sort of
presence—something close, filling, and active—was such that it did
not matter whether he could be seen or not. Johnson stresses that
his work was never visible to anyone not directly affected by its
operation. He found his patients in dark places, "in misery's darkest
cavern," among outcasts, people who lived in isolation and seclu-
sion. And even they were not affected by what was visible in him:
the important thing, rather, was the secret activity of his drugs.
Thus Johnson writes: "His vig'rous remedy display'd / The power of
art without the show." The remedy worked inside the patient's body
where it was invisible; when the patient grew well, his body became

the visible sign or "display" of the drug's potency. In this way, a fluid bond linked the image and Levet's active presence such that one could be inferred from the other; but at the same time the difference between them was preserved, and Levet's presence remained independent of and prior to its representation in the patient's body. His value was hidden, like the talent in the parable; the difference was that it was active in its invisibility, and in fact rendered the visible a secondary effect. This is why Johnson says it was not wasted: "sure th'Eternal Master found / The single talent well employ'd."

Levet's distance is not just a matter of perception; Levet was also, socially and personally, a marginal figure. Johnson suggests in the third stanza that he was the sort of person high society would have spurned—or did spurn—and the phrase "Obscurely wise and coarsely kind" indicates that his abilities were limited. It is unclear how to separate this shambling awkwardness of his from his metaphysically more impressive capacity for being full and present, but that passage in the stanza suggests that Johnson does not want to identify the two notions with each other, though he blurs them together. He says: "Nor, letter'd arrogance, deny / Thy praise to merit unrefin'd." Johnson here expresses a traditional and familiar suspicion of "letters," to which, just as traditionally, he contrasts Levet's homely fullness of presence; as such, these lines go along with the poem's prevailing dismay about representation. But it is clear from the fact that Johnson makes this appeal at all, and from the cool decorum of his style—the formal-sounding use of apostrophe and the inversion of the noun-adjective order—that he is writing from inside the literary establishment, and that he is, in however self-critical or tentative a fashion, committed to it. His severity is that of a writer with so much authority over his readers—whom one takes here to be his colleagues—that he can afford to antagonize them. This is why the passage feels, in an affectionate and tactful way, condescending; and the feeling is reinforced later, when Johnson imagines the paternal fondness of the "Eternal Master" for Levet. However much Johnson admires Levet, he does not write as if he ought to abase himself or repudiate his work, which belongs to the world of "letter'd arrogance." Levet was better than everybody else in that he did not think of himself as being better; what Johnson's condescending tone suggests—and this gives the poem its astringent pathos—is that Levet was right: he really was not better than anyone else.

All of which makes for the poem's peculiarly hushed and allusive style of moral rumination. It would have been jarring, both because Levet sinks away before representation, and because he is so little, to present him as an icon of moral authority; but at the same time he interests Johnson as an exemplar of the moral quality of resignation. In the *Life of Savage,* when Savage tries to make something aristocratic from his endurance of the world's neglect and abuse, the emptiness of his rhetoric is evident. In the poem, Johnson wants to praise Levet's resignation to the same neglect and abuse; but he must not make Savage's error and heroize Levet. He accordingly keeps the moralizing quiet, muffled in the form of implication; he never editorializes. He characterizes Levet mainly by making pointed negative comparisons: he says that Levet was "unrefined," that he mocked no summons, disdained no fee, made no pause, left no void, never counted the days and nights. The negatives reproach the reader (identified as "letter'd arrogance"), but the reproach hides as part of the description: thus its force is fractured—one cannot say that Johnson is aiming at one thing—and at the same time both Levet and the reader seem shadowy, half-realized figures on the fringes of the negation. A moral atmosphere permeates the poem mistily, sustained by the indeterminate movement between concrete terms and resonant abstractions ("left no void"), a movement which makes the difference between them seem minimal. The insistent use of personification has a similar effect. Thus the phrase "His virtues walk'd their narrow round" completely blurs the distinction between metaphorical description and literal narration.

The ambiguous jostling together of realistic specificity and allegorical abstraction not only tones down the poem's moralizing impulse but also sets it free: for if the allegorical language is subdued by the language of biography, it also permeates it and detaches it from its referents in the real world. It would be impossible to say how much of what Johnson says is true. The border between the life and the representation dissolves—because, ironically, of Johnson's sense that a public representation of Levet is bound to be a distortion. As a measure of the pull of figurative language in the poem, and of the subsumption of the life into it, consider the last stanza:

> Then with no throbbing fiery pain,
>   No cold gradations of decay,
> Death broke at once the vital chain,
>   And free'd his soul the nearest way.

The negatives imply that Levet had a choice about and was in some way responsible for the character of his death. Not in a way that could be explained in terms of intention or biology: Johnson is not suggesting that Levet planned his death, and he is not thinking about how balanced his diet was. He is working out the figurative correspondence between resignation, the prevailing theme of Levet's existence, and death. Death's quickness and painlessness here correspond to what Johnson has said about Levet's practice and person; and by invoking the terrible extravagance of the alternative deaths Levet could have suffered, he infuses the death he did in fact die with an ethical character, as though it were an example of moderation. Even the rhythm moralizes the passage, for the use of antithesis and the rocking alternation of negatives sustain the faintly hypnotic lilt of the rest of the poem and thus seem to refer to the same kind of experience. The bizarreness of this account of Levet's death tells us that Johnson is dreaming here, perhaps satisfying some wish. Presumably it quiets his own terror of the deathbed; it might also reflect a desire to tie the poem off thematically, for to the extent that Levet is master over his death, he would appear to authorize the transition from lived experience to those exemplary images left behind at his death. In any case, it appears that it is the blurring of descriptive and moralizing language that facilitates this slide into fantasy.

Such a slide would not have been likely if Levet's resignation could be construed as a public virtue, since in that case Johnson would not have had to restrict the moral commentary to the form of implication. As it is, this moment of fancy measures the extent to which the poem's rhetoric has abandoned realism, has had to abandon it, in order to hold onto its didactic purpose. The poem can engage in moral generalization only symbolically: the virtue it praises is necessary only because there is no felt, material connection between the character and the society at large. His marginality expresses a divorce between personal and social experience; it involves a breakdown of the ability to generalize concretely from particular lives. Moral reflection can bridge that gap rhetorically; but if it tries to incorporate into its meditation the fact of marginality, it becomes clear that its language, like Savage's, is just a way of talking.

Five

Probability and Conjecture

Johnson's moral thought is closest to eighteenth-century social theory when it becomes probabilistic. Contemporary philosophers had not fully developed a probabilistic approach to the description of masses, but they had begun to do so;[1] and probabilistic argument appears likewise scattered throughout Johnson's writing. There is a mechanistic dimension to such argument that puts it at odds with traditional moral argument. As we have seen, when Johnson argues for the consoling power of moral reflection, he contrasts it with gambling. But he also evinces much uncertainty about that consoling power; and at the same time probabilistic thinking seems to have helped allay his anxiety in the face of runaway multiplicity. He turns to it, therefore, ambivalently, but often. In his argument about moral thought and gambling, he appears unconscious that he makes the two activities sound similar; it is as if he were stumbling into a probabilistic attitude despite himself. But elsewhere, the influence of probabilistic thinking is deep and elaborate.

Numbers seem to have been comforting to him. Hester Piozzi reports that, whenever Johnson felt his imagination "disordered, his constant recurrence was to the study of arithmetic" (Piozzi 200). Once during the period of near-breakdown he went through in the 1760s, she found him in his room "in the midst of a series of elaborate calculations. He was taking the national debt, computing it at 180 millions sterling, and then calculating whether it 'would, if converted into silver, serve to make a meridian of that metal, I forget how broad, for the globe of the whole earth' " (200). In other bad times, he applied similar calculations to this own projects. A couple of weeks before he left Oxford, in despair, debt-ridden, unable to finish his degree, he made a sort of chart "in which he outlines for himself what reading a certain number of lines per day (10, 30, and so on up to 600) would amount to in a week, then a month, then a year" (Bate *Samuel Johnson*, 106). Bate notes that Johnson kept making charts like this throughout his life, even when he was old and famous.

This habit was a form, Bate suggests, of Johnson's "anticipative imagination," his strategy of allaying a fear of the unexpected by considering beforehand all of the turns of fortune that might befall him. His calculations and charts warded off the unexpected specifically by breaking experience—even the "globe of the whole earth"—into comparable units, a move which would put the future into a predictable and knowable relation to the present and past. In his writing, in more sober and circumspective moments, he argues that such schemes for regulating the flow of events are generally doomed, if not to fail, then at least to struggle against a mass of unpredictable contingencies. Instead of warding off the unexpected, such schemes give it occasions in which to unfold itself—in the form, for example, of the laziness that keeps one from sticking to a schedule, or of unavoidable external distractions, or of unforeseen confusions. But since Johnson is less interested in preventing the unexpected from happening than in warding off its shock effects, he concentrates most of his attention not on forming plans, but, according to Bate, on figuring out in advance all the ways things can turn out. Johnson's mobility as a writer—the multiple perspectives he adopts in arguments, his constant movement from propositions to qualifications, his enumerative turn of mind—can be seen as a defensive effort, in Bate's words, "to overlook nothing, to take it all into account beforehand" (107). By covering all the possibilities in his mind, he does not get around the impossibility of predicting the future, an impossibility he often gloomily calls attention to in his writing, but at least things that come unpredicted do not come to him completely unexpected, or at any rate do not come as a shock he is unprepared for.

In a discussion of the development of consciousness in the modern city, Benjamin argues that this kind of defense has a significant cultural consequence: it undermines the sense that experience is rooted in tradition. Citing Freud, Benjamin argues that consciousness is opposed to memory: instead of retaining experiential impressions, it protects one against stimuli. It dissipates "the effects of the excessive energies at work in the external world" by registering them in the place of "other systems," in which, Freud writes, stimuli leave "permanent traces as the basis of memory."[2] Paradoxically, consciousness wards off shocks by registering them, as if registration were simultaneously an erasure. Benjamin suggests a way of understanding this: consciousness protects us against stimulation by isolating impressions. The more efficiently it is "alert as a screen against stimuli . . . , the less do these impressions enter experience . . . , tending to remain in the sphere of a certain hour of one's life" (117).

This effort poses a problem for consciousness. Though it parries shocks by isolating them, it also must somehow anticipate them, somehow repeat and contextualize them. "According to [psychoanalytic] theory, fright has 'significance' in the 'absence of any preparedness for anxiety.'" This is why accident victims have repeated nightmares about their accidents: they are "endeavour[ing] to master the stimulus retroactively, by developing the anxiety whose omission was the cause of the traumatic neurosis" (115). The dilemma of consciousness is how to isolate shocks but at the same time stay prepared for them; circumscribe them without suppressing the premonitory halo of anxiety whose absence transforms them from excitement into trauma. Consciousness does it by regarding time as pure chronology, what Benjamin calls "empty" time, a transparent medium in which all moments are equivalent, abstract, and interchangeable. When time is "empty," anticipation and isolation go together, for present, past, and future are equivalent to the same extent that every moment is discontinuous with every other. Assigning an experience a place in this chronology isolates it by con-textualizing it. "Perhaps the special achievement of shock defense may be seen in its function of assigning to an incident a precise point in time in consciousness at the cost of the integrity of its contents" (117).

The shocks of big-city life make people rely heavily on conscious-ness as a defense, Benjamin argues. He cites the newspaper and the mechanization of labor under industrial capitalism as products of experience organized around "empty" time; he might have cited Johnson's "anticipative imagination" as well. By the nineteenth cen-tury, Benjamin argues, the shock defense had become so prevalent a psychic mode that writers began to rebel against it, lest experience in general lose the "integrity of its contents."

For Johnson, though, whose hold on the shock defense seems tenuous and desperate, embracing the desolating effects of con-scious structures such as anticipation and routinization can still appear as a grave moral obligation. Far from trying to disrupt their constant and oppressive operation, he struggles to maintain the spell of these structures against a persistent barrage of tempting arguments for letting them go. For him their dismalness does not tell against them; it is only an occasion for moral effort, one effort among others to endure something awful that cannot be made any better. Nor does he try to legitimate these structures by fabricating some continuity between them and the sort of experience whose contents Benjamin would consider still to be intact. Johnson's ac-count of consciousness is consistently grim: he hates routine, and he writes hopelessly and incessantly about the despair of a fully com-prehended and anticipated world, a world bereft of novelty. But still he remains faithful to the demands of routine and anticipation. In what follows, we will consider how they appeal to him, and what they cost him.

––––––

Benjamin outlines some literary corollaries to the shock experience, particularly "the replacement of the older narration by information" (113). Information, which Benjamin associates with newspapers, is not assimilated by readers as part of their own experience: rather it "isolate[s] what happens from the realm in which it could affect [their] experience" (112). Items of information are unconnected to one another and do not imply a personal relation between those who receive and those who purvey the information, nor a relation to its content. Such items do not "enter 'tradition.'" They seek to "convey a happening *per se.*" Storytelling, on the other hand, "one of the oldest forms of communication," embeds an event "in the life of the storyteller in order to pass it on as experience to those listening" (112). Benjamin does not try to show that information replaced storytelling at a particular period, but he links this movement to the experience of big cities and to the technology of mechanical reproduction. Following Benjamin, Benedict Anderson argues that the conception of the nation, a community of so many members that it cannot be apprehended in any direct experiential way, arose along with the experience of what Benjamin calls "homogeneous, empty time," the only mode of experience open enough to contain the dispersion of vast anonymous crowds without having recourse to the idea of the sacred. In the Middle Ages, Anderson points out, it was common to represent biblical stories as if they happened in the present, not by way of imagining them in "modern dress," but rather because the link between past, present, and future was conceived to be essentially a timeless relation of prefiguration and always already consummated fulfillment. Anderson argues that this conception of simultaneity gave way to homogeneous, empty time, the conception of simultaneity as "temporal coincidence . . . measured by clock and calendar," first with the development of the printing press and then with the rise of "two forms of imagining which first flowered in Europe in the eighteenth century: the novel and the newspaper."[3] The printing press contributed to the rise in power of vernacular languages, a movement which destabilized the status of Latin as a sacred language, and at the same time it established a common language between speakers whose dialects were otherwise typically unintelligible to one another. In so doing, it crystallized a mode of figuring or imagining community that was unavailable before (47). But the newspaper not only constructed a writing-oriented figure for community, it assembled experiences on the basis of their association in calendrical time: in newspapers events appear together because they share the same date (37).

In Johnson's writing, then, we can detect his preoccupation with information not only in his massive efforts of accumulating facts—the dictionary and the edition of Shakespeare—but also, following Anderson, in the disconnectedness of his periodical essay writing. He contrasts essay writing with the compilation of a "system of science," an extended work elaborated according to "long trains of consequence," by pointing out that periodical writing follows only the law of the calendar: every "day calls afresh upon [the writer] for a new topick, and he is again obliged to choose, without any principle to regulate his choice" (R 184, 5:201–2).

Johnson's tasks of information gathering, like his charts and calculations, evidently helped him pull himself together; at least we know that he never brought himself to start working except under the pressure of a deadline. But on the other hand, he is conscious of a disorienting tendency in such constraints. Though Benjamin argues that structures of consciousness protect one against the "excessive energies" of city crowds, they seem to dazzle Johnson with a sense of these crowds by putting him into an obsessively enumerative relation to the world. Writing for a daily deadline makes the world disintegrate into a chaotic mass before his eyes: "It is indeed true, that there is seldom any necessity of looking far, or enquiring long for a proper subject [for a periodical essay]. Every diversity of art or nature, every public blessing or calamity, every domestick pain or gratification, every sally or caprice, blunder or absurdity, or stratagem of affectation may supply matter to [a writer] whose only rule is to avoid uniformity" (R 184, 5:202). Not only does this mass churn before him with incomprehensible variety, but it scatters his thinking across the expanse of its apparent boundlessness: as one contemplates it, "it often happens, that the judgment is distracted with boundless multiplicity, the imagination ranges from one design to another, and the hours pass imperceptibly away till the composition can no longer be delayed" (5:202). Thus, while periodical writing isolates and disjoins events to keep them from entering experience, it also intimates the possibility of their endless proliferation, and the mechanism that is supposed to protect one from the crowd also turns it into a determining figure of one's thought. Understanding an event (or in Johnson's case, choosing a topic) requires that it be placed in the right context—which is also understood to mean a complete context—but who can tell what that would be with a newspaper, where decontextualization is the governing principle of organization? This is a problem with any reading, but newspapers thematize the problem in their layout. It would be a particularly disconcerting problem for someone like Johnson, to the extent that he defends himself against shock, as Bate says, by "taking it all into account beforehand." What happens when trying to take it all into account beforehand draws one instead into the midst of "boundless multiplicity"?

The only way to stop this proliferation is by some arbitrary intervention; and this is what Johnson describes. However boundless routine and information gathering may be potentially, in practice they invariably run up against contingent disruptions. In the case of periodical writing, deadlines make it necessary finally to choose topics at random; by a kind of violence, one reduces the multiplication of possibilities, but only at the cost of giving way to chance determinations (R 184, 5:202).

To absorb the jolts and disappointments of the accidents produced by chance, Johnson adopts a line of thought about mass phenomena according to which accident is an inevitable concomitant of multiplicity. Accident appears part of a predictable pattern. In the "Preface" to the *Dictionary,* for example, he apologizes for the "wild blunders . . . from which no work of such multiplicity was ever free" (259). In the *Life of Pope* he says of Pope's representation of himself as translating fifty verses of *The Iliad* a day: "According to this calculation, the progress of Pope may seem to have been slow; but the distance is commonly very great between actual performances and speculative possibility. . . . Perhaps no extensive and multifarious performance was ever effected within the term originally fixed in the undertaker's mind" (3:117). The train of thought here is familiar and sensible enough, but also complicated inasmuch as it involves a shift from the logic of experience to a logic of probabilistic calculation. Slowdowns and blunders are linked to the multifariousness of an undertaking, but the linkage is not directly causal and not even determinate. Even if the complexity of a long task necessarily brings problems in its wake, it is on the other hand also the case that any specific problem is contingent: inevitably there are lapses in a routine, but saying this does not explain why there are these lapses in particular. Instead of a causal relation which would establish a continuous relation between a general principle and particular experiences, this argument allows the specific to lapse into mere contingency, and it searches for structures of necessity on the level of the aggregate. This disjunction is what makes the reasoning probabilistic. The argument is statistical: mistakes are understood as a percentage of a large work, lapses in routine as a margin of error.

Through this blurring of a specific event's contours, a conceptual shift takes place from which one can only return to specific events in the empiricist mode of taking a random sample. The literary effects of this mode can be attractive: it becomes possible to spin out long, desultory lists of random experiences and still give the impression that the writing is driving at a coherent point. For instance, in the "Preface" to the *Dictionary* Johnson gives the following account of the kind of unexpected contingencies that can beset a writer: one must remember, he says,

> that a writer will sometimes be hurried by eagerness to the end, and sometimes faint with weariness under a task, which *Scaliger* compares to the labours of the anvil and the mine; that what is obvious is not always known, and what is known is not always present; that sudden fits of inadvertency will sometimes surprize vigilance, slight avocations will seduce attention, and casual eclipses of the mind will darken learning; and that the writer shall often in vain trace his memory at the moment of need, for that which yesterday he knew with intuitive readiness, and which will come uncalled into his thoughts tomorrow. (259)

Similarly, in the *Life of Pope* he treats particular obstructions to routine as random and virtually imperceptible: "Indolence, interruption, business and pleasure all take their turns of retardation, and every long work is lengthened by a thousand causes that can, and ten thousand that cannot, be recounted" (3:117).

The pleasure of such lists lies in the feeling that they can include anything and yet not have to organize their contents in any over-arching, systematic way. At best, they are organized strictly accord-ing to rhetorical force: the randomness of their elements allows Johnson to think entirely in terms of surface effects. But this kind of writing is available to him because of the frame of probability around them; and if this stylistic mannerism is prevalent in his work, that is an indication of how deep-seated probabilistic think-ing is with him. It even affects his moralizing style. What readers call his "generosity," his willingness to put himself in the place even of someone whose faults he is criticizing, manages to accompany a severe code of rights and wrongs because he never moves to specific cases without crossing a probabilistic space that attenuates any ex-perience's particularity. Even when any given fault might have been avoided, it is hard to judge it harshly if one imagines at the same time that *some* quantity of faults is inevitable.[4]

In the "Preface" to the *Dictionary* Johnson excuses the errors he has committed as "human" errors: the "Preface" gets its effect by drifting between a remark at the beginning about "the imperfection of human things" (235) and the pathos-laden image of the frail lexicographer, laboring under the shadow of death, incapable of sustaining his efforts with the machinelike regularity asked of him (259). It is of course a traditional Christian idea to define the "hu-man" as a liability to error. But Johnson's "Preface" reconceives that idea in terms of factorylike labor, as though Christian faith and humility would take the form of a rigorous adherence to a dehu-manized, mechanical routine. One can gauge the peculiarity of this confluence of rhetorical modes by considering the pathos Johnson brings to bear on the topic of Pope's failure to follow his translation schedule: "Perhaps no extensive and multifarious performance was ever effected within the term originally fixed in the undertaker's mind. He that runs against Time has an antagonist not subject to casualties" (3:117). It takes a minute, given the solemn and funereal overtones of this last sentence, to realize that Johnson is only trying to explain that sometimes Pope was lazy. But for Johnson, the failure to follow a routine is not only a contingent matter of laziness: it is also, on the contrary, an inevitable failing which marks the vanity of human undertakings. The discourse organized around the disjunction between these two notions of failure—as contingent and as inevitable—is that of probability and statistics. Human vanity is the margin of error, statistically defined, in any large work. Consequently, the "human" becomes a conceptual wild card: it personifies the array of elusive contingencies which upset the unfolding of routine—likewise any effort to gather information—and whose inexplicability the language of statistics derives its power from presupposing. It personifies the random, the nonconceptual, and ultimately the unrepresentable.

Presumably one attraction of this statistical conception of the "human" would be that it is more coherent—less "perplexing and suspenseful"—than the "boundless multiplicity" Johnson has to contend with when he is aimlessly gathering information and has not yet taken the risk of making a decision. Furthermore, to the extent that it motivates his catalogs of random examples, catalogs in which he indulges the pleasure of multiplying surfaces and discontinuities, it is responsible for one of his most seductive literary practices. But at the same time it radically marginalizes a personal conception of the "human"—much more radically than the gestures of self-sacrifice he diffidently analyzes in his writing about marginal characters like Richard Savage and Dr. Levet. Martyrdom is a gesture in which the self asserts its power: in it, self-sacrifice becomes self-aggrandizing. But when the human becomes a statistical representation of a routine's inexplicable disruption, its marginality undermines the concept of specific experience *in general* and, as Benjamin says, destroys the "integrity of its contents." This discourse derives its power precisely from regarding the moment and the personal axiomatically as random and contingent and examining the patterning of large masses. It assumes from the outset that the task of describing the general is disconnected from the task of describing the particular.

The results of this thinking are apparent in a poem like "The Vanity of Human Wishes," where personal agency is a generalized construct akin to a statistic. The figures in this poem are not "typical" in Georg Lukács's sense;[5] there's no dialectical interplay between the particular and the general, no attempt to make the universal concrete. Their identity is merely figurative, and the construction of the figure is authorized only by generalization. Since no construction of identity in this discursive register refers to personal experience, empirically inconceivable figures are possible: it recalls the kind of language that allows a family to have 2.5 children. In such a discursive mode, it is apparent that the marginalization of the self can have nothing to do with the gratifying transfers of power and structures of consolation available in, say, the martyr's experience of self-sacrifice. The self is not marginal here because one has given up its power: it is marginal in that it is the figurative construction of some bureaucratic imagination.

———

Probabilistic thinking helps organize the overwhelming multiplicity of crowds into a graspable form, but it does so at the expense of some notion of "humanness." In the preface to his edition of Shakespeare, Johnson writes about the poise he thinks one needs to sustain this loss.

This essay revolves around a version of Benjamin's distinction between storytelling and information. In this case the distinction is between original composition and editing, and ultimately between Shakespeare and Johnson. Editing, as Johnson sees it, is essentially and radically marginal. It is marginal with respect to original composition, which comes first in order of literary priorities and which moreover controls most of the power available in literature. Literary power for Johnson means the power not only to please but to produce emotional involvement in general, a power without which literature becomes empty drudgery. It is what we read for—so much so that even a badly garbled edition of a great work impresses readers, according to Johnson, almost as strongly as a good edition. Literary power confirms the universality of our humanness. This is why Shakespeare is supreme. On the one hand, he integrates the general and the particular: his characters are universally recognizable but at the same time individual and distinct. On the other, his universal popularity guarantees that some notion of humanness is

universal and that it constitutes a standard of judgment. He wards
off the fear that judgment is mere opinion, mere cultural prejudice.
Johnson imagines the movement from original composition to
editing in temporal terms: the period of critical commentary follows that of composition as a stage of decline, a stage of decayed
power, as if the literary scene were organized entropically, like a machine perpetually winding down. Commentary provides virtually
nothing of value to anyone reading for the sake of the text's power—
Johnson even urges readers who are coming to Shakespeare for the
first time to ignore the notes. Commentary is intended instead for
readers concerned with "exactness" of understanding (7:111). But
since Johnson imagines such readers as cold and jaded scholars who
have lost their susceptibility to the text's power, the propagation of
critical commentary appears as a circulation of waste: worthless
services provided to those who would be incapable of receiving a
service of value. What makes its basic economy skewed and eccen-
tric is that, even despite its virtual worthlessness, editing is nevertheless exorbitantly difficult. Critics need extensive knowledge of
texts, and their judgment in cases of emendation must be excep-
tionally fine; meanwhile they also engage in vicious battles with one
another, and the accumulation of their learning ceaselessly prolifer-
ates; but at bottom virtually nothing is at stake. Johnson speculates
that there is some logic of compensation in this: "Perhaps the light-
ness of the matter may conduce to the vehemence of the agency;
when the truth to be investigated is so near to inexistence, as to
escape attention, its bulk is to be enlarged by rage and exclamation"
(7:102).

This wretched and virtually meaningless activity is to be understood, though, as an approach to the way things really are: as some
kind of advance on original composition, which is the source of
energy and meaning, the center of literary activity, but also a mi-
rage. For Johnson entropy has two incompatible meanings which
allow him to conceive of marginality as the worst of both worlds: it
means loss and decay, the fall from meaning, but it also implies that
what has been lost never really existed. Thus, Shakespeare could be
"read, admired, studied, and imitated, while he was yet deformed

with all the improprieties which ignorance and neglect could accumulate upon him" (7:111), but still: "It is to be lamented, that such a writer should want a commentary; that his language should become obsolete, or his sentiments obscure. But it is vain to carry wishes beyond the condition of human things; that which must happen to all, has happened to Shakespeare, by accident and time" (7:112). In other words, Shakespeare is as strong as ever despite all the deformities heaped upon him by time, but nevertheless he has also declined irremediably (as "must happen to all"). Editing presides over this scene where no one is singled out, not even the greatest geniuses. Because Shakespeare thrives, editing is a worthless falling away from his immortal vitality, but because he is decayed, editing remains necessary and becomes representative of the powerlessness that disables everything human, even the works of Shakespeare. This contradiction constitutes its radical marginality: even though it is worthless, it must nevertheless be pursued in all its poverty. Original composition is doubly displaced in this line of thought. Not only is its power doomed to decay: from the outset it lacks authority, for, as Johnson represents it, it is blind to the inevitability of the decay of power in general. But editing is not blind to this necessity; and this is the sense in which it is the more lucid of the two pursuits.

Conjecture comes into this argument like the moment in *Rambler* No. 184 where Johnson has to choose a topic after scattering his thoughts over a boundless multiplicity of possibilities. He has to fill in a gap that the pursuit of information has left him with—in this case, he has to repair a corruption in Shakespeare's text; in the other case, he has to say something coherent—but he can only do it by making a random move, an arbitrary decision or guess, which exposes him to error (7:109). To contain the problem of error (which he cannot fully resolve), he relies on the probabilistic nature of conjecture: he dispels the threat of making a mistake by pointing out that he is only guessing. When a proposition is marked as a conjecture, it is immediately freed from the risk of error. As Johnson says, "There is no danger in conjecture, if it be proposed as conjecture" (7:108).

But having taken these precautions, he is absorbed with the question of what they have cost him. The unguarded mode of conjecture he has renounced leads one to make mistakes, but it is also the only task available to an editor that appears to bring one back into contact with the pleasure of original composition and literary power. According to Johnson, the "allurements of emendation are scarcely resistible"; and its primary allure is the promise of originality, a promise so gratifying that it seduces editors away from their responsibility to the dessicated principle of correctness: "Conjecture has all the joy and all the pride of invention, and he that has once started a happy change, is too much delighted to consider what objections may rise against it" (7:109).

The risk of making a guess at random presumably adds to the flutter of excitement here, a flutter one can also hear in that *Rambler* essay where Johnson speaks of choosing an essay topic at random: "necessity enforces the use of those thoughts which then happen to be at hand [and the] mind rejoicing at deliverance on any terms from perplexity and suspense, applies herself vigorously to the work before her" (5:202). Another remark about conjecture suggests what would link originality to risk taking. When Johnson is attacking critics for covering up the flimsiness of their conjectures under a mass of irrelevant verbiage, he makes a surprising claim for the possibility of a certain kind of easy, unmistakable critical mastery: "I have always suspected that the reading is right, which requires many words to prove it wrong; and the emendation wrong, that cannot without so much labour appear to be right. The justness of a happy restoration strikes at once, and the moral precept may be well applied to criticism, *quod dubitas ne feceris*" ("When in doubt, don't"; 7:108–9). Apparently for a certain masterful criticism, conjecture manages not to be doubtful: its justness "strikes at once." But at the same time, *all* conjectures are doubtful, even those of a critic of "wonderful sagacity and erudition": "when [a critic] succeeds best, he produces perhaps but one reading of many probable, and he that suggests another will always be able to dispute his claims" (7:109). The allure of mastering conjecture would lie in the fantasy of reconciling these two imaginings of chance. It is the allure of the professional gambler: constantly exposed to chance, but skilled at dealing with it. It would likewise be the allure of the writer of original compositions, whose innovation recklessly breaks with past models, but nevertheless evinces the confidence that comes from obedience to a rule.

Most of Johnson's account of editing is an attempt to cut his losses by weakening this link between unguarded conjectures and original composition. The link between them is merely apparent, he argues. Conjecture is structured not like original composition but like editing and information gathering. It has "no system, no principal and axiomatical truth that regulates subordinate propositions"; it is repetitive inasmuch as the critic's "chance of errour is renewed at every attempt"; it subjects the critic to the domination of random influences: "an oblique view of the passage, a slight misapprehension of a phrase, a casual inattention to the parts connected, is sufficient to make him not only fail, but fail ridiculously" (7:109). Johnson writes generally in a harsh, satirical tone about the critics who have engaged in conjecture; but his distaste for them has less to do with moral disapproval than with a cold recognition that their efforts at mastery have only gotten them lost in a crowd of bunglers.

> To dread the shore which he sees spread with wrecks, is natural to the sailor. I had before my eye, so many critical adventures ended in miscarriage, that caution was forced upon me. I encountered in every page Wit struggling with its own sophistry, and Learning confused by the multiplicity of its views. I was forced to censure those whom I admired, and could not but reflect, while I was dispossessing their emendations, how soon the same fate might happen to my own, and how many of the readings which I have corrected may be by some other editor defended and established.
>
>   Criticks, I saw, that other's names efface,
>   And fix their own, with labour, in the place;
>   Their own, like others, soon their place resign'd,
>   Or disappear'd, and left the first behind.   Pope.
>
> (7:109)

What is striking here is the conjunction of futility and anonymity: the wrecks are particularly terrible because there are "so many" of them, and the "struggling" recalls the turmoil of a blind, seething crowd. The awfulness of undergoing the "same fate" as everyone else is not so much that it involves making mistakes, but that it is the *same* fate. It is equivalent to the wretchedness of repetition that goes with editing, only here these critics lack even the dignity of having known what they were getting into. This is the advantage, such as it is, that Johnson has over them.

He marks his conjectural emendations as such by putting them in the footnotes, outside the body of the text, where they will not be mistaken for solid information. This is a strange kind of composition: one can neither take it nor leave it. It is no sooner offered than withdrawn. If one begins to incorporate it, one has to reject it at the same time; but since it is in the text, neither can one dismiss it altogether. Johnson seems to want his writing to take a reader through a detour like the wishes granted by demons in fairy tales: after it's over, they leave you where you were before. As long as the magic cancels itself out, like imaginary numbers in physics, one can make room for any extravagance: "Since I have confined my imagination to the margin, it must not be considered as very reprehensible, if I have suffered it to play some freaks in its own dominion" (7:108).

But Johnson is clear about the cost of writing in this mode. If he has cut his losses by dispelling the temptation of unguarded conjectures, he is still acutely conscious that he is engaged only in a choice of evils. Since his conjectures are marginal, they have no power. At most, they have the power of sapping the text's power. They mark its absence; and they fragment it by pointing to a corruption without guaranteeing that it is a corruption. In a dull, unproductive way, they invite suspicion, but they neither let the corrupt passage go nor supplant it with a substitute. Instead of staying confined to the margins, they minimally *multiply* the text. But Johnson gets no power over the text or the reader in this process. The most he can say for himself is that he did the *correct* thing, and this assessment is purely negative, like the remark in the "Preface" to the *Dictionary:* "It is the fate of those who toil at the lower employments of life, to be rather driven by the fear of evil, than attracted by the prospect of good; to be exposed to censure, without hope of praise; to be disgraced by miscarriage, or punished for neglect, where success would have been without applause, and diligence without reward" (234). He would have betrayed the obligation to give correct information if he had put his conjectures in the body of the text; but putting them in the margins earns him no praise, the less so given that they exist strictly in order to cancel themselves; and since correctness is a value one embraces only after one no longer has contact with literary power, even the negative virtue of not betraying it seems to be no virtue at all. Johnson himself appears to be left halting within the doubleness of these constraints. He insists that the need to be correct is an imperative obligation: "The greater part of readers, instead of blaming us for passing trifles, will wonder that on mere trifles so much labour is expended, with such importance of debate, and such solemnity of diction. To these I answer with confidence, that they are judging of an art which they do not understand" (7:107–8). But to be in the right on this issue does him no good; the obligation he is faithful to is pointless and wasteful: "[I] cannot much reproach [those readers] with their ignorance, nor promise that they would become in general, by learning criticism, more useful, happier, or wiser" (7:108).

Conclusion

This book has been arguing that Johnson is a moral skeptic. He is concerned with the limitations on our knowledge and our powers of acting. He evokes the predicament of judging without criteria. Moral reflection is necessary just where nature provides no law; the crowd is of concern because it prevents us from substituting public consensus for nature as a foundation for judgment. The crowd multiplies contexts for judgment, breaks the rhetorical link between the general and the particular, and marginalizes personal action.

Johnson's skepticism maintains itself in part through his reluctance to formulate generalizations about society and politics. He finds public affairs too confused and complex for understanding and suspects that most talk about them is ill-informed posturing; and as I said at the outset, he is for this reason attractive to literary critics who feel both a pressure to politicize their work and a doubt about the good of doing so. What about the politics of this skepticism, though? It is a familiar notion that skepticism promotes conservatism. Should we argue that this is true in Johnson's case, that his diffidence about political schemes and his preoccupation with the haplessness of individual action recommends an attitude of passivity and resignation to the status quo?

A discussion of skepticism by J.-F. Lyotard suggests that the answer here might be no.[1] Skepticism should promote passivity and conservativism, it is commonly argued, because it reminds us that we know little, and when one knows little, it is imprudent to act. Lyotard observes, however, that according to a long tradition of political theory, knowledge cannot in any case provide the basis for just action. Philosophers in this tradition—Lyotard speaks of Aristotle, the Sophists, Nietzsche, and Kant—do not believe, as for example Plato and Marx do, that philosophy can formulate the idea of a just society, authorize it as an object of knowledge, and derive from it a program of action. They argue that we have only opinions about justice, not knowledge, and for this reason discussion about action is itself essentially a form of action, specifically of persuasion and rhetoric. No opinion has the certainty of knowledge, but some opinions are better than others: they are more persuasive.

Lyotard innovates on this tradition by linking it to the Wittgensteinian concept of language games. Discussion of political action and social justice, he argues, is not only not scientific and certain; it does not even play the same game as the discourses of knowledge do. Justice is linked with prescriptive language. Prescriptions—commands, prayers, advice, and the like—do not concern themselves with knowledge; they are not "predicative" (22); they cannot be either true or false. For this reason, Lyotard asserts, they cannot be derived by means of implication "from discourses of knowledge, whose function is to state the truth, and that are determinable with respect to truth or falsehood" (22). "This passage from one to the other is, properly speaking, unintelligible" (22)—as unintelligible as, for example, the passage between the rules for checkers and the rules for chess.

Since prescriptive utterance is primary in questions of justice, it does not become more just or less—or even more or less *likely* to be just—as it moves closer to or further away from knowledge. On this view, there is no intrinsic reason to derive a conservative ideology from a skeptical theory of action. Conservatism discourages change on the ground that, since we are blind in political matters, the effects of change are necessarily uncertain; the status quo is at least knowable. But from a Lyotardian perspective, this sounds merely like a confusion of different language games with each other, an injunction to evaluate a prescription according to how closely it resembles a statement of knowledge. The conservative recommendation not to act is itself an action, like any other prescription; it has to be judged as such, none the less for its attempt to adhere to a criterion of certainty.

The desire to base judgments on criteria is certainly not surprising, but in matters of prescription, Lyotard argues, criteria are bound to be mere imitations. As a skeptic, Johnson seems to have intuited this circumstance; so he writes often about judging blindly and plays ambivalently at following rules whose authority seems provisional or illusory. His conservatism, I will try to show, represents a version of this recourse to imitation certainty. It does not so much follow from his skepticism as offer an imaginary consolation for it.

————

Donald Greene has argued that Johnson should be identified politically as a skeptic in the manner of David Hume or H. L. Mencken.[2] Johnson was a Tory in the early sense of the word, according to Greene: that is, not a reactionary supporter of authoritarianism, but a disaffected political outsider like the small landowning gentry of the early eighteenth century, who did not so much espouse a political position as grumble at the positions of the politicians in power (20). Most political schemes, Johnson said to Boswell, are laughable things. Taking this as his skeptical motto, Johnson (argues Greene) exposed political self-deception, dishonesty, and, above all, *cant:* in his reports of the parliamentary debates in the early 1740s, he contrasted the self-serving rhetorical excesses of the opposition to the modest, measured, and substantial self-defense of Walpole (127–29); in his articles of 1756 on English foreign relations, he swept aside talk of lofty national ideals and tersely identified the economic motives behind England's foreign policy (160–63; 168–70); and in his pamphlets on the popular uprisings in England and America during the 1770s, he rejected the romantic idealism of the opposition's leaders and insisted on the mundane realities and unavoidable inequities of the British scheme of political representation (204–19). Johnson's instincts were individualistic and skeptical (253); he did not so much favor a return to an all-powerful monarchy as he deplored the deceptiveness of the ruling party's seeming egalitarianism. In Greene's portrait, Johnson emerges as a political critic, a gadfly, an anticolonialist, a supporter of education for the lower classes, and a staunch believer in the obligation of all to exercise their personal intelligence and judgment about political issues.

The main weakness in this argument concerns political skepticism generally: that is, the argument does not settle the objection that Johnson's skepticism promoted his political conservatism. Johnson makes the connection clear, for example, in "The False Alarm."

> Governments formed by chance, and gradually improved by such expedients, as the successive discovery of their defects happened to suggest, are never to be tried by a regular theory. They are fabricks of dissimilar materials, raised by different architects, upon different plans. We must be content with them as they are; should we attempt to mend their disproportions, we might easily demolish, and difficultly rebuild them.[3]

Greene is right that Johnson finds political schemes laughable things, and that he regards most political discussions as exercises in cant. We know little about how economic and social systems work; they do not rest on a coherent set of interlocking logical principles. "It seems to be almost the universal error of historians to suppose it politically, as it is physically true, that every effect has a proportionate cause . . . but the operations of life, whether private or publick, admit no such laws."[4] But this admission of frailty, though it motivates Johnson's criticism of the politically powerful, directs his attack especially against the schemes of innovators. "Change, says *Hooker,* is not made without inconvenience."[5] We must be content with things as they are because in our blindness we may worsen our lot in the attempt to improve it.[6] Greene is by no means unaware of this trend in Johnson's thinking; on the contrary, he summarizes it succinctly: "On the basis of experience (the skeptical conservative finds) the probability is that the confusion arising from an upheaval in the familiar ways of doing things, absurd as they may be, will produce a greater total of unhappiness than will be balanced by the amount of happiness to be produced by the proposed reform. This is a highly rational, not an irrational, attitude" (254). But for Greene, this does not suggest that "Johnson is *advocating* anything except clear thinking" (246).

Johnson was a kind of gadfly, but it remains true that he was also authoritarian.[7] He regarded the political fabric of England as an irresistibly necessary scheme of subordination in which the mass of people must live in obscurity in order to support all that was "splendid, conspicuous, or exalted" (R 145, 5:9). Spiritual and cultural refinement is a blessing stolen from the power of material toil; only by freeing up a small elite for reflection and study can civilization raise itself up from the constraint of brute necessity; and therefore the many must be made to take over the work of the few. Culture is an artifice made possible through the imposition of elitist power on a society otherwise egalitarian.[8] Greene tries to redeem Johnson's notion of subordination by glossing it as the "social division of labor"—as if it were a horizontal principle designating who undertakes which task (153, 177); but clearly, Johnson means to affirm a hierarchical principle of natural selection. "On his favourite subject of subordination, Johnson said, 'So far is it from being true that men are naturally equal, that no two people can be half an hour together, but one shall acquire an evident superiority over the other' " (*Life* 2:13). Social discrimination is natural or at any rate inevitable. The lowly have not the same personal value as the highborn: when told that a poor man who shot a lord for trampling him with his horse had claimed to be protecting his honor, Johnson retorted angrily: "A poor man has no honour" (*Life* 3:189).[9]

Johnson's tone becomes strident and clamorous when he contemplates the prospect of popular rule and the reorganization of the political pyramid. Of the American colonists, he says their talk of liberty and enslavement is hysterical, and then he adds acidly: "This contest may end in the softer phrase of English superiority and American obedience."[10] No longer merely obedient to their sovereign, the Americans are to confess their inferiority to the English as a people: Johnson here drops any pretense of resolving a political dispute equitably and pants to see the colonists soundly beaten and humiliated. In the pamphlet on the Falkland Islands he strikes a similar note: "To fancy that our government can be subverted by the rabble, whom its lenity has pampered into impudence, is to fear that a city may be drowned by the overflowing of its kennels" (10:386). It is a measure of the difficulty of thinking of Johnson as antiauthoritarian that Greene says of this passage only that public demonstrations in the eighteenth century were not democratic but rather symptomatic of the need for a police force (211). What I want to call attention to and think about, rather, is the virulence of this tone. It is uncharacteristic of Johnson; in the passage on the Americans, he even means to chide them for *their* tonal extremism; but no one who equates people with overflowing sewage brimming with dead animals can claim to be taking the rhetorical high ground.

The tone suggests strain: Johnson's views in his political pamphlets are contradictory and in some respects irrational; and ultimately, it appears, they strain at the problem posed by the radicalism of his skepticism, which his conservatism tries to contain and repress. It is not self-evident that his skepticism should give rise to his conservative views, despite the claims of the Hume-Burke tradition. At least two other, unskeptical ideas figure into his argument to yield that result.

First, though Johnson claims that society is formed by chance, made up of dissimilar materials, and "never to be tried by a regular theory," he also insists that society is ordered by a scheme of "regular subordination" (10:421). Modern Europe, he argues, represents a time of order by contrast to the middle ages; by the time Columbus sailed, "fluctuations of military turbulence had subsided, and Europe began to regain a settled form, by established government and regular subordination" (10:421). In earlier times, Columbus would have found his way to "some discontented lord" who would have built and seized ships for him. But by the 1490s, the age of "vagrant excursion and fortuitous hostility" was past. The regularity of modern society gives it a coherence different from the crazy quilt character Johnson ascribes to it when he calls it a structure made of disparate materials brought together by chance. The subordination of colony to mother country, for example, is like the relation of a limb to a body (10:425). This is true of colonies generally in the modern era, by whose "wiser laws and gentler manners, society [is] more compacted and better regulated" (10:420).

The morass of local customs, personal experiences, historical accidents blocks systematic reasoning about government in some passages of Johnson's argument, but gives way in others to an affirmation of the integration, rationality, and legibility of the present order. With modern times, the relation between government and subjects became one of mutual recognition and attention: government "protected individuals, and individuals were required to refer" their well-being to that of the government. Now, instead of living for himself, every "man is taught to consider his own happiness as combined with the publick prosperity" (10:420). In a colony's charter, this political coherence is not only unlike the mass of local customs of "governments formed by chance" but is directly opposed to it: thus, when a charter is repealed, "the whole fabrick of subordination is . . . destroyed, [and] the society is dissolved into a tumult of individuals" (10:425). So here the materials of a culture accumulated over centuries are not primarily responsible for holding society together; rather, that cohesion depends on the authority of a charter.

But this then suggests an essentially unitary source of social order and a theory that government could, after all, be explained by an appeal to basic principles. The significance of this is that it indicates how highly regulated, coherent, and legible Johnson is prepared, at times, to find government. He wavers: sometimes social order is a vast, complicated mystery that humbles all inquirers; sometimes it seems as simple as authority and obedience. A slide happens here, such that the first view comes to support the second, even though they contradict each other. Starting with a feeling of humility with respect to historical change and the vastness of political problems— this is an epistemological humility, in other words—Johnson shifts into an attitude of humility with respect to established authority, as if it were not likely that the politicians were as blind as we are. Epistemological self-effacement here is tricked into playing the part of political subservience and acquiescence.

Just as social order is alternately a crazy quilt and a regular system of subordination, so attempts to change the social order threaten, sometimes, widespread ruin and at other times make no difference at all. Johnson's general pronouncement on innovation is that "we might easily demolish [social fabrics], and difficultly rebuild them" (10:328). Because governmental power is strong, the "rabble" do little damage; but Johnson vividly evokes the wreckage that would spread if they were not suppressed. They are blindly self-interested: "these kings of *Me*," he calls the American colonists. Government is impossible without an institution invested with sovereign authority; but the American colonists and the rabble supporting Wilkes presume to dictate to the sovereign the laws they are willing to obey. "They allow to the supreme power nothing more than the liberty of notifying to them its demands and necessities," a claim which, Johnson observes, "supposes dominion without authority" (10:418). They are the latest in a long parade of agitators for the destruction of hierarchy. They have disturbed the nation's quiet for years; their "original principle is the desire of levelling"; and they are "only animated under the name of zeal, by the natural malignity of the mean against the great" (10:341). They remind Johnson of the uprising of the "vilains" during the Hundred Years' War, an insurrection which posed a greater threat than the warring lords posed to one another. When the peasants took up arms, "the knights of both [England and France] considered the cause as common, and, suspending the general hostility, united to chastise them" (10:341). Wilkes's supporters are drunken, ignorant, clamorous, destructive, gross, indecent, savage, cruel; the American colonists are a Hydra, and this thought makes one "naturally [consider] how the Hydra was destroyed" (10:414).

But on the other hand, no one—not the rabble, not a dictator— can much affect the everday course of life. The rabble are harmless not so much because government authorities put their rebellions down as because it is almost impossible for any action to transform the basic quality of life. Changes in the form of government matter little, Johnson argues. "I would not give half a guinea to live under one form of government rather than another. It is of no moment to the happiness of an individual. [T]he danger of the abuse of power is nothing to a private man" (*Life* 2:170). To Joseph Baretti, Johnson wrote: "The good or ill success of battles and embassies extends itself to a very small part of domestic life: we all have good and evil, which we feel more sensibly than our petty part of public miscarriage or prosperity" (21 Dec 1762); and he added this famous couplet to Goldsmith's poem "The Traveller": "How small of all that human hearts endure/ The part which laws or kings can cause or cure!"[11] He felt not only that party politics and parliamentary debate had little impact on society at large, but also that even general social upheaval, even widespread violence, left the essential supports of social order unshaken. In the pamphlet on the Falkland Islands, he deplores the wasting effect of war on the populace, but observes that it leaves large-scale social forms untouched: "Thus is a people gradually exhausted, for the most part with little effect. The wars . . . make . . . slow changes in the system of empire" (10:371). Social innovators can involve the people in general misery, but when the smoke clears, virtually nothing will have changed.

Both of these general positions—that innovation may easily demolish what we have with so much difficulty erected, and that innovation may spread misery without changing the basic unhappiness inherent in society—elaborate coherent imaginings of the consequences of blindly taking political action; but as general propositions, they are incompatible, and the fact that they both attract Johnson suggests that they may hold his attention more for rhetorical reasons than analytical ones. They allow him to write in a variety of interesting tones: he is lurid, restrained, sardonic, and drily deliberative by turns. Sometimes he evokes the wreckage of a noble social order, sometimes the futile clamor of a violence that accomplishes nothing. Albert Hirschman identifies these as two of three major rhetorical modes in reactionary writing: one mode pursues the drama of a "jeopardy thesis"—the thesis that innovation threatens earlier gains; the other mode elaborates a "futility thesis"—that innovation is much ado to no purpose.[12] The futility thesis promotes a tone of cool, penetrating irony; the jeopardy thesis sounds massively learned, humane, and laden with pathos. As rhetorical modes, they help organize and shape apprehensions about politics that feel otherwise unwieldy, general, and perplexing. One of them responds primarily to the notion that society follows a scheme of regular subordination, so that the threat of easy demolition seems plausible; and the other corresponds to the quilt conception of society, a conception which distributes authority to so many disparate, manifold, and local sources, that no attack on society could be comprehensive enough to transform it significantly. But given that both views are so entrenched and elaborated in Johnson's writing, it cannot be right to attribute his conservativism simply to his skepticism. The question, rather, is how the two work together, and whether they are not, like "jeopardy" and "futility," at odds with each other.

Readers of Johnson often call him an empiricist; and they show that in political matters he insisted on the importance of material fact over system-building. They are right about this, but it is important to stress that his empiricism repeatedly has a moralizing flavor; he offers it as an exemplary display of intellectual work; his empiricism is always presented as a triumph over the temptation to idealize; and consequently, the factual or real tends to blur into the abstract form of any figure that frustrates the idealizing impulse. The political consequences of this appear in Johnson's three main topical pamphlets of the 1770s. Empiricism here means skepticism; it presents a general and emblematic challenge to the desire for systematic political theory. The common target of all three pamphlets is the notion of "right," or an ideal ground for political authority. "The False Alarm" is about the turmoil that arose when the House of Commons claimed that Lutterel, who had gotten fewer votes, had beaten John Wilkes, who had gotten a majority, on the grounds that Wilkes, convicted of libel and obscenity, was ineligible to sit in Parliament.[13] Wilkes's supporters complained that the Commons was violating a principle of the constitution and unjustly arrogating to itself a power to make law and impose representatives on the people against their will. The American colonists argued a similar case a few years later, and "Taxation No Tyranny" attacks their complaint about the taxation of those who were unrepresented in Parliament. Johnson argues that these complaints idealize authority; they call for a systematic justification of political sovereignty that ignores its essential and irremediable arbitrariness.

Sovereignty is not based on a principle of right but only on a conceptual necessity or tautology, that is, that a legislative power which cannot require obedience is no power at all. Government does not derive its power from a prior right either in the form of divine investiture or a social contract. Johnson dispenses with such political fictions. Governmental power is not to be justified, it is merely a fact; it is posited, and it ceases to exist once it is disregarded. "The first laws had no law to enforce them, the first authority was constituted by itself" (10:322). This paradox is Johnson's central "fact": it is a rhetorical loop that identifies fact particularly as an obstruction to a kind of reasoning, to the appeal to a transcendental ground. It appears in other places in Johnson's writing. In the "Preface" to the *Dictionary* he says that certain words are the simplest; the synonyms he uses to define them are harder than they are. And in *Rambler* No. 8, he argues that moral thought is possible because the mind is not always absorbed in immediate tasks: thought is moral because it does *not* have a ground, not because it does; it wanders in boundless expanses of imagination like matter floating in space. The repetition of this train of thought suggests that it attracted Johnson as a literary artifact, a story that satisfied some aesthetic impulse; and this contributes to the feeling that fact, for him, means above all a figure in a moral train of thought about imagination and idealism.

Fact is a figure, in other words, for skepticism, for the apprehension that we know little or nothing. What makes it a fact is its opacity, its power to block speculation. We "see every day the towering head of speculation bow down unwillingly to grovelling experience" (10:328). So Johnson conceives of political institutions as brute fact, and on the other hand, he sees them as fragile symbolic artifacts. They block us, humble us, disappoint us: we must obey them against our wishes. But at the same time, they symbolize this very obligation as a general spiritual predicament. Institutions are contingent and paradoxical: *merely* empirical. The paradoxes in them are important to Johnson as figures for their contingency, their "mere"-ness. Parliament cannot be regulated by a higher power because power has to be lodged somewhere; and therefore it is drawn into the loop of self-regulation of which Wilkes's supporters complain. Similarly, Parliament has a "right" to tax the American colonists simply because that power is in the nature of governmental authority. Johnson approves evidently of parliamentary representation of public needs; but he also says of the Americans that, even if they had a representative, they would still be taxed, and therefore their clamor is to no purpose. Political representation is valuable, and yet it affects nothing. It performs an obscure symbolic role: it initiates action for people negotiating the vast empty space of politics. It is a pretense of regulation where political events happen arbitrarily.

Johnson explores this theme for its rhetorical wealth most effectively in his "Thoughts on the Falkland's Islands." Again, what fascinates him is the spectacle of authority without right, authority where all claim to right is inconceivable. Under such circumstances, authority can only be posited, not justified, and consequently claims to "regularity" and "order" appear to be contingent perspectives on chance. The Falkland Islands lay off the coast of South America in a region generally acknowledged to belong to the Spanish, but the islands themselves were discovered by British sailors, or so the British claimed. Johnson emphasizes that the first sighting, if that is what it was, happened in a storm: the core of his discussion is that there was no original scene of discovery (10:351). The Spanish were in the region first, the English may have seen the islands first; between these claims, there can be no principled adjudication. Eventually the two countries came into conflict over the islands, after a British garrison erected a fortress there and the Spanish drove them off. The English insisted on staying as a matter, not of right, but of honor; and the Spanish finally, "for whatever reason," agreed to let them, but without ceding their own right of sovereignty (10:366). The strength of Johnson's pamphlet lies in its evocation of the hobbling, frail ricketiness of this solution, and the irremediable obligation of resting satisfied with it. The opposition faction, led by Junius, clamored for war to wrest the right to the islands, free and clear, from the Spanish. Johnson replies: "But when we have obtained all that was asked, why should we complain that we have not more? When the possession is conceded, where is the evil that the right, which that concession supposes to be merely hypothetical, is referred to the Greek Calends for a future disquisition? Were the Switzers less free or less secure, because they had never been declared independent before the treaty of Westphalia? Is the King of France less a sovereign because the King of England partakes his title?" (10:367).

Already in the sequence of these questions, he gives the impression that the situation in the Falklands is exemplary. He also gives that impression in his account of the lives the soldiers led on the island. The island is presented as an emblem of the moral topic of material reality and its conflict with the imagination. The garrison was sent there by Lord Egmont, a man, we are told, given to "romantick projects and airy speculations" (10:356). The first surveyor of the islands, Captain Byron, described them as fertile, strategically placed, and rich in ore; this description then turned out a wild flight of fancy, and the second surveyor, Captain Macbride, discovered the islands to be desert and barren. Johnson pictures the garrison "shrinking from the blast [of Atlantic storms] and shuddering at the billows" (10:358), for some time untroubled by rivals since the object of their conquest was worthless.

> This was a colony which could never become independant, for it could never be able to maintain itself. The necessary supplies were annually sent from England, at an expence which the Admiralty began to think would not quickly be repaid. But shame of deserting a project, and unwillingness to contend with a projector that meant well, continued the garrison. . . . That of which we were almost weary ourselves, we did not expect any one to envy; and therefore supposed that we should be permitted to reside in Falkland's Islands, the undisputed lords of tempest-beaten barrenness. (10:358)

The mingled pathos, irony, and sense of ramifying absurdity not only recall Johnson's moral essays but constitute the passage itself as a moral essay. Johnson wants to resonate as widely here as anything in *Robinson Crusoe;* the passage recalls Addison's description of primary imagination as the world bereft of color and form, like the desert into which an enchanted knight awakens when the spell has been broken.[14] Samuel Beckett loved to read Johnson; and it is easy to imagine him liking this passage.[15]

But it is exemplary not only of moral truths and of a moral apprehension of something like the "human predicament": it also serves as a figure for the pamphlet's main political theme—the obligation to accept the contingency of political authority, which exercises power without indisputable right. Just as no transcendental principle of right justified the soldiers' presence on the island, so nothing on the island itself supported their existence there. They literally had no ground. Nothing grew in the island's barren soil: "A garden was prepared, but the plants that sprung up withered away in immaturity. Some fir-seeds were sown; but though this be the native tree of rugged climates, the young firs that rose above the ground died like weaker herbage" (10:358). Nothing took root in the soil, and the wind blew constantly; Johnson says that the garrison lived in a "wooden blockhouse built at Woolwich, and carried in pieces to the island" (10:361), a grim and funny detail to remind us that the soldiers were no more rooted in the soil than the withering shrubs. They stayed there merely by virtue of their having found themselves there. The barrenness of the ground, its powerlessness to anchor anything, was like the absence of right in the political conflict. Just as that conflict forced the English to content themselves with the mere fact of possession, so the soldiers stayed on the island through sheer labor. "*Nil mortalibus arduum est.* There is nothing which human courage will not undertake, and little that human patience will not endure. The garrison lived upon Falkland's Island, shrinking from the blast" (10:358). They sound like Richard Savage. Like his contrivances, their labor is a kind of theft which steals an existence from nothingness.

The mingling of concrete political commentary and abstract Godotesque evocations of the absurdity of human life gives the pamphlet its fizzy literary attractiveness. This is the style of political reflection Johnson enjoys: while examining a concrete, "empirical" topic of current affairs, he suffuses the writing with the pathos and glamorous generality of metaphysical speculation.[16] He does it by making the concept of fact the object of moral reflection. The general lesson is that one must be specific. The paradoxical entanglement of general and specific helps forge another main analogy for the island: the soldiers' rootlessness is not only like the English lack of right, but also like political power in general—like the power of Parliament to expel members against the public's wishes and to tax Americans without giving them political representation. Johnson makes this general point in the Falkland's pamphlet: "If sovereignty implies undisputed right, scarce any prince is a sovereign through his whole dominions; if sovereignty consists in this, that no superiour is acknowledged, our King reigns at Port Egmont [in the Falklands] with sovereign authority. Almost every new acquired territory is in some degree controvertible, and till the controversy is decided, a term very difficult to be fixed, all that can be had is real possession and actual dominion" (10:367).

After laying out this argument about the arbitrariness of political power—its basis not in principle but in brute fact, its lack of systematicity—Johnson turns to attack the pro-war faction in England, and ultimately what he calls the "rabble." This, then, is at least one concrete example of the relation between his skepticism and his authoritarianism, and so an opportunity to say something specific about that relation.

The main objection to the faction here, and to the rabble in the other two pamphlets, is strikingly like the remarks Johnson has just made about sovereignty: they cannot justify themselves. The rabble intrude into politics without having an "interest" in it. Like "right," "interest" is consistently absent from the political controversies Johnson writes about. No one ever had an interest in claiming possession of the Falklands. "The advantage of such a settlement in time of peace is, I think, not easily to be proved. For what use can it have but of a station for contraband traders, a nursery of fraud, and a receptacle of theft?" (10:354). The islands are "a few spots of earth, which, in the deserts of the ocean, had almost escaped human notice" (10:350). The English held onto them primarily out of shame that they had ever wasted time on them (10:358). How much less interest, Johnson continues, would there be in going to war for them? The rabble has agitated for war primarily at the instigation of Junius, the rabid newspaper orator, and his faction. The power of rhetoric, playing upon ignorance, has inflamed their passions, which oppose their interests. In this case, their interest lies in leaving the Falklands alone; as far as Johnson is concerned, this was true for all the disputants from the start.

"The False Alarm" suggests that the people have *in general* little or no interest in political affairs. They have complained that the Commons infringed upon their liberties in the Wilkes affair; but they do not actually feel an injury. Their complaint is abstract and theoretical, driven by passions, not by real needs. Johnson imagines an "enlightened mind" of "higher rank" addressing the supporters of the Wilkes petition: "You are appealing from the Parliament to the rabble, and inviting those, who scarcely, in the most common affairs, distinguish right from wrong, to judge of questions complicated with law written and unwritten, with the general principles of government, and the particular customs of the House of Commons" (10:338). Political affairs are complex and theoretical; but the people should not meddle in them if their interest is not direct and personal. "[You] are shewing them a grievance, so distant that they cannot see it, and so light that they cannot feel it" (10:338). The people cannot see or feel this issue; it will emerge that this means that they have no "interest" in it. "Interest" belongs to conflicts in a person's everyday life, to matters of immediate need like food and housing.

Johnson then explains that the rabble come to imagine that they have more extensive or intangible political interests when they are worked on by outside forces of oratory: "how, but by unnecessary intelligence and artificial provocation, should the farmers and shopkeepers of Yorkshire and Cumberland know or care how Middlesex is represented?" This may seem like a merely local and reasonable observation: in some sense, perhaps, those farmers and shopkeepers had no direct concern in these matters. But Johnson goes on to claim that the idea of "interest" here (the interest of the lower orders) is apolitical in general. "[It] is the duty of men like you [the petitioners], who have leisure for enquiry, to lead back the people to their honest labour; to tell them, that submission is the duty of the ignorant, and content the virtue of the poor; that they have no skill in the art of government, nor any interest in the dissensions of the great" (10:338–39). Political dispute here is a matter for those who have "leisure for enquiry." That means, on the one hand, that it is the province of the upper classes (the "dissensions of the great"), but, on the other hand, that it is a vagrant, imaginative undertaking, a kind of useless sport like literature or like setting up a garrison in the Falklands. Some political issues, though presumably not all, act primarily upon what Johnson elsewhere calls the "adscititious passions." They fire the imagination without concerning natural needs; they work through writing, oratory, newspapers; they take the form of "unnecessary intelligence and artificial provocation." In their arbitrariness and their appeal to the imagination, they link the theme of absence of interest with that of the absence of right.

Sometimes, but not always, Johnson exposes the absence of interest as an objection to a political position, as in his condemnation of the rabble here. He deplores the Wilkes controversy because the stakes are merely imaginary: "one part of the nation has never before contended with the other, but for some weighty and apparent interest. If the means were violent, the end was great" (10:343). In the civil war and the Jacobite insurrection, at least something important was at issue. In the Wilkes case, the controversy involves no "apparent interest" at all. Similarly, he wonders at British supporters of the Americans: "Passion has in its first violence controlled interest" (10:412). But it is generally true, too, that political debates insistently baffle attempts to distinguish the trivial from the serious, the imaginary from the real, and the passions from the interests: "To proportion the eagerness of contest to its importance seems too hard a task for human wisdom. The pride of wit has kept ages busy in the discussion of useless questions, and the pride of power has destroyed armies to gain or to keep unprofitable possessions" (10:349). Later he writes: "The caprices of voluntary agents laugh at calculation. It is not always that there is a strong reason for a great event" (10:366).

Following Johnson's argument about the "adscititious passions," some of which are to be "regulated" rather than suppressed, it seems as though certain political passions, though devoid of "interest," might require "regulation" rather than suppression. This would seem especially true in political cases where the consequences could be great but, because of the complexity of the question, one could not see them clearly, or where the consequences were far enough off that one could only have an imaginary and theoretical feeling for them. In *Rambler* No. 9 Johnson argues that it is valuable for inventors and projectors to have a prejudice in their own favor even though prejudice is irrational; for it prods them to keep working when the outcome of their work remains uncertain (3:50). Since political affairs involve the massive uncertainty and complications evoked in Johnson's pamphlets, political reflection would seem to require, similarly, an "adscititious" passion, like prejudice, to drive it forward. In this sense, even good political reflection will involve "cant," theatrical emotions, "unnecessary intelligence and artificial provocation." The task is to regulate these effects, not suppress them.

But Johnson unequivocally wants to silence the rabble's uproar about these controversies. His tone, as I said, is strident; at times he is attractively scornful and sarcastic, at others just ugly. If he were simply concerned that the Junius faction might drive England into war with Spain or that the Middlesex controversy might set off widespread rioting, his anger might be understandable. But since he insists at the same time that the popular clamor is meaningless and ineffectual, the acid in his tone seems wild and excessive. He sounds not just concerned, but vindictive and repressive: he wants to chop off Hydra's head and drown the vermin in the kennels.

His authoritarianism here does not work together with his skepticism; instead it seeks to suppress the vagrant unpredictability represented by the crowd. He is reactionary in this argument not so much because he is unsure what the best policy might be as because the rabble embodies a vast murky apprehension that in many ways political questions are unaccountable. The essays begin by saying that political facts do not conform to principles; they "laugh at calculation," they overwhelm us; we can only learn them through painful experience, and no one situation tells us how to act in the next: in politics we must always improvise, stagger from expedient to expedient. And the essays end by heaping abuse on the rabble for their ignorance about political matters, their unpredictability, their lack of principle, their temptation to venture into the "dissensions of the great," matters which are not their concern. Thus, in their general drift, the essays transfer the messiness and multifariousness of politics, which in the beginning they admonish us to accept, onto the rabble, which they then castigate with vehement repugnance.

In the Falklands pamphlet, this transfer happens through a chain of metaphors. Johnson says that politics is unlike physics: small actions can produce disproportionate effects (10:366). This notion reappears in the figure of the destructive vapors that "silently" and "invisibly" killed thousands of British soldiers in recent conflicts in Spanish America. Heroic romance pictures war as a combat between comparable antagonists: victory is a sign of greater strength. But in fact war is unheroic and laughs at calculation. It has "means of destruction more formidable than the cannon and the sword. Of the thousands and ten thousands that perished in our late contests with France and Spain, a very small part ever felt the stroke of an enemy; the rest languished in tents and ships, amidst damps and putrefaction; pale, torpid, spiritless, and helpless . . . at last whelmed in pits, or heaved into the ocean, without notice and without remembrance" (10:370–71). Thus were fleets "silently dispeopled and armies sluggishly melted." By contrast to heroic fiction, this is real war; the contrast is like the one between a theoretical view of politics and an empirical one. War's factuality appears in its subjection of individuals: just as the hero of romance becomes, in real war, a statistic, so the order and subjectivism of a theoretical perspective must give way to the incalculability and impersonality of material reality. Again, empiricism here is skeptical; the appeal to fact is not an appeal to personal experience but to what thwarts the personal, like paradoxical reversals of causal relationships, the defacement of the individual, and the dissipation of solid experience into vapor. Here Johnson is arguing that the faction is dangerous because it fails to see that this vaporishness is the real nature of war and more generally of political reality. But at the same time they are responsible for the vapors, and soon they turn into vapor. War enriches a few businessmen and politicians "whose equipages shine like meteors and palaces rise like exhalations" (10:371). These grim financiers laugh at slaughter while "adding figure to figure, and cipher to cipher" (10:371).

But then it emerges that not an elite, but rather the rabble is primarily responsible. They are led by Junius, the pamphleteer, whom Johnson deplores above all because, by remaining anonymous, he makes himself invisible. Like Jack the Giant-Killer in his "coat of darkness," Johnson complains, Junius "may do much mischief with little strength" (10:376); because he is invisible, he is "out of the reach of danger" (10:377). He is a vapor of rhetorical tricks. Like invisible damps, he has an effect completely out of proportion to his power: "he has had the art of persuading when he seconded desire; as a reasoner, he has convinced those who had no doubt before; . . . as a patriot, he has gratified the mean by insults on the high. . . . It is not by his liveliness of imagery . . . that he detains the cits of London. . . . Of stile and adornment they take no cognizance. They admire . . . contempt of order, and violence of outrage" (10:377). Thus, he has no literary gift, no persuasive power; he merely repeats what the rabble already think, and so volatilizes them into a destructive force of outrage. He is formidable and powerless like them—he is a notion whipped up out of thin air. What "folly has taken for a comet that from its flaming hair shook pestilence and war, enquiry will find to be only a meteor formed by the vapours of putrefying democracy, and kindled into flame by the effervescence of interest struggling with conviction; which after having plunged its followers in a bog, will leave us enquiring why we regarded it" (10:378). That bog is like the kennels to which Johnson consigns the rabble at the end. Either they float in them or are the water in them. Johnson ridicules the notion that the rabble might subvert the government, but the ugliness of his ridicule gives the impression that he is wildly lashing out. Why is he so vitriolic about an enemy that poses no danger? The metaphorical pattern suggests that it is because the crowd has here come to mean the incalculability of politics, the sort of incalculability that perverts causal relations, reduces heroes to statistics, and silently drowns cities in invisible vapors.

Undertakings like the Falklands garrison are analogous to Johnson's style of political reflection. Johnson generalizes from specifics as gingerly and with as little right as the fortress stood on the Falkland soil. The sense of cant might well have troubled Johnson; a few years after the "Taxation" pamphlet he blew up in a rage when Boswell and some others made a case for the colonists which he could not answer (*Life* 3:315–16). His scorn for Junius as a writer must have contributed to the bitterness of his attack on the rabble, and it is only one passage among others that suggest that he felt, as a writer, an uneasy identification with the crowd as an idle meddler in political affairs. As a writer, he was disinterested, and he advertised his disinterest as a badge of honor. "I have great merit in being zealous for subordination and the honours of birth," he said to Boswell; "for I can hardly tell who was my grandfather" (*Life* 2:261). Boswell says that, as a writer, Johnson was entitled to address all classes in the same way; he never bowed to lords and ladies, for his literary genius put him outside class categories (*Life* 4:116). This freedom of position or hierarchical mobility was enviable and delightful (and according to Barrell, much political theory of the period argued that accurate political reflection could emanate only from such a position), but it entailed the danger of whimsicality and fancifulness, just as the rabble went wrong when oratory loosed it from its anchorage in interest.

Johnson is anxious not to seem uninvolved and academic. He does not pretend in the pamphlets to be above the disputes he surveys; instead, he contrasts the humble empiricism of his perspective with the grandiose romanticism of his opponents. While he weaves passages of moral reflection about the state of man, he condemns the opposing faction for their failure to stick to specifics. He begins the Falklands pamphlet by observing how ungratifying to the imagination it will be: "the writer to whom this employment [is] assigned, will have few opportunities of descriptive splendor or narrative elegance. Of other countries it is told how often they have changed their government; these islands have hitherto changed only their name. Of heroes to conquer, or legislators to civilize, here has been no appearance; nothing has happened to them" (10:350). By contrast, the discoverers and settlers of the islands were given to "romantick schemes" and the Junius faction to notions drawn from "heroick fiction" (10:370). The supporters of Wilkes have taken a wild and fanciful alarm; and America as a whole, found by Columbus, who was a "wild projector" (10:421), and Vasco da Gama, who fired Europe "with boundless expectation" (10:421), embodies escapist fantasy. The colonists try to work on the British with theatrical emotion—tales of sentiment and terror (10:413–14)—and they "scorn the limits of place" (10:430).

Several times Johnson makes them reenact metaphors of the imagination he has formulated in other places. When they admit they are British subjects not in a state of nature, he says: "These lords of themselves, these kings of *Me,* these demigods of independence, [thus] sink down to colonists, governed by a charter" (10:429). The passage has a rhythm familiar in Johnson, as in this passage from the "Preface" to the *Dictionary:* "From these dreams I was to awaken at last a lexicographer" (252). The rhythm and echo help measure how much Johnson personalizes the American conflict, how much he sees the colonists in a drama he has staged long before, and how much they represent fears about the imagination he has long nursed in his reflections about writing. He repeats this rhythm at the essay's end. He supposes that, after a British victory over the colonists, "those who now bellow as patriots . . . will sink into sober merchants and silent planters, peaceably diligent, and securely rich" (10:453). Here they sink, as he does, but they sink into silence, into peaceful indifference to political debate. The trick of his pamphlets is to give the impression that he has sunk into peacefulness too, even though he presumes to break silence. He accuses them of imaginative excess; in "The False Alarm" one can hear another similar echo: "The choice of delegates [in British elections] is made by a select number, and those who are not electors stand idle and helpless spectators of the commonweal, 'wholly unconcerned in the government of themselves' " (10:427). In *Rambler* No. 8, explaining how the soul daydreams because "we contrive in minutes what we execute in years," he writes: "the soul often stands an idle spectator of the labor of the hands, and the expedition of the feet" (3:41). The rabble would like to believe that government can directly undertake helpful political programs, but in fact government is slow, difficult, and cumbersome. The echo is surprising because it reverses the presumed process of giving direction: government is not the soul that directs the body, but rather the opposite. Elsewhere, he affirms that ordering is its role; but when the soul is a figure for disorderly daydreaming, then it is equated with the crowd.

Johnson's political pamphlets begin complex and skeptical, but they end simple and authoritarian. Along the way, the crowd takes onto itself the burden of confusion which Johnson begins by attributing to political questions in general, the confusion that comes from recognizing no absolute right of authority in any political sovereign, and from finding in political reflection the unavoidable cant of a rhetoric driven not by direct experience and personal interest but by imaginative theory and abstract passion. The crowd is revealed to be prey to imagination and passion; it craves overly neat pictures of reality (in war) and enjoys nothing but disorder and destruction; it intervenes clumsily in the dissensions of the great, who alone are qualified to reflect on political questions; and it talks in cant, though it has no liveliness of imagery and no care for "stile and adornment." The murkiness of the English-Spanish conflict simplifies itself into a conflict between Johnson and Junius; the paradox of parliamentary representation reduces to the simple opposition between English superiority and American obedience. These dynamics are disappointing. They make the pamphlets less interesting and less likable than Johnson's other writing. But they offer one way of arguing for a disjunction between Johnson's skepticism and his authoritarianism. It is hard not to admire his acumen in seeing how little we know about politics and society at large; and it is encouraging to feel that our admiration for him need not expose us to the charge of irresponsibility through acquiescence and passivity. In the pamphlets Johnson is disappointing only for not pursuing his skepticism far enough. When he pursues it further—in his other writings about crowds—he strikes a tone that one wants to hear: informed, energetic, gloomily resigned to personal limitations, and still intensely aware of the need for change.

Notes

Introduction

1. The first major expressions of this trend include, of course, Bertrand Bronson, "Johnson Agonistes," in *Johnson Agonistes and Other Essays* (Cambridge: Cambridge UP, 1946), 1–52; and W. J. Bate, *The Achievement of Samuel Johnson* (New York: Oxford UP, 1955). Bate's biography, *Samuel Johnson* (New York: Harcourt, Brace, and Jovanovich, 1976), elaborates on ideas presented in the earlier Johnson book.

2. See, e.g., Bate's *Achievement,* which celebrates Johnson's "empirical grasp of the immediate problem" (31). Philip Davis, in *In Mind of Johnson: A Study of Johnson the Rambler* (Athens: U of Georgia P, 1989), writes of Johnson's "practical reasoning" (130–47).

3. See, e.g., Joseph Wood Krutch, *Samuel Johnson* (New York: Henry Holt, 1944), 76.

4. See Isobel Grundy, "Samuel Johnson: Man of Maxims?" in *Samuel Johnson: New Critical Essays,* ed. Isobel Grundy (London: Vision P, 1984), 13–30; Robert Folkenflik, *Samuel Johnson, Biographer* (Ithaca: Cornell UP, 1978); William Vesterman, *The Stylistic Life of Samuel Johnson* (New Brunswick: Rutgers UP, 1977); William Edinger, *Samuel Johnson and Poetic Style* (Chicago: U of Chicago P, 1977).

5. Leo Damrosch, *Samuel Johnson and the Tragic Sense* (Princeton: Princeton UP, 1972): "In the fate of Peyton, of whom we know nothing more than the little Johnson tells us, we receive an intimation of the fate of all men, which of course includes our own" (99). Arieh Sachs, *Passionate Intelligence: Imagination and Reason in the Work of Samuel Johnson* (Baltimore: Johns Hopkins UP, 1967): "The true aim of art is precisely the aim of the moralist: to show 'the uniformity in the state of man.' A recognition of this basic uniformity is supremely important because by providing a release from the tension of self and subjectivity it leads to salvation" (79). Paul Alkon, *Samuel Johnson and Moral Discipline* (Evanston: Northwestern UP, 1969): "Not only as a reporter but whenever he picked up his pen, Johnson sought to achieve universality" (4).

6. See Bate; Edinger; Folkenflik; Vesterman.

7. "The literary 'individual' who remains merely an individual has not been adequately comprehended. . . . The concept of 'general nature' exists, then, to distinguish the kind of universality-through-particularity that we acknowledge in such triumphs of realism as Emma Bovary, Gabriel Conroy, and Leopold Bloom, characters which reflect no limitation of moral intelligence—no striving for effect, no personal investment, no ulterior motive—on the part of their authors, but whose humanity emerges with their autonomy, their freedom to be so fully and concretely what they are. Johnson found these qualities in the characters of his favorite authors Homer, Shakespeare, and Richardson, whose 'invisibility'—the sign of negative capability and of undistorted perception—compares with that of Flaubert and Joyce" (91–92).

8. Jean Hagstrum, *Samuel Johnson's Literary Criticism* (Minneapolis: U of Minnesota P, 1952): "[N]ature as the source of art may be viewed under two aspects: nature as life, reality, or particular experience; and nature as some kind of general order. . . . Both these conceptions, which may seem to be contrary and antithetical, but are not, I think, contradictory, are accepted as equally valid by Johnson" (56–57). The two aspects become available to the artist strictly through experience. Nature has a general order but not a Platonic or Neoplatonic sort. "If . . . nature as reality and truth does not disclose itself, how is it made available to art? Only through the continuing and deepening *experience* of the artist, who must unveil nature since she will not do it for herself" (74).

9. "[F]ew moralists have lived as he did—so close to the edge of human experience in so many different ways. . . . Hence the ring of authority in so much that he says. We know that he has gone through it himself at genuine risk or peril, and that his assimilative nature—most aroused when turned to the personal problem of 'how to live'—has digested it. . . . [W]hat distinguishes him . . . among moralists . . . is the incredible range. . . . Nothing is left untouched. And yet, when he is through, we find ourselves discovering—what we had never realized before to the same degree—how much of a piece humanity is, and how common the lot we all share in such short time as we have" (*Samuel Johnson,* 297). Johnson does it through "compression": the "aphoristic power, which makes him so quotable, was . . . to be a distinguishing feature of his prose style, both written and spoken. The desire to 'manage' experience by compressing it into condensed generality is something we have been noting in him since the verse exercises he wrote as a boy in Stourbridge" (*Samuel Johnson,* 291).

10. For instance, "the psychologizing of the theme [of vanity] is organically built into the approach" in "The Vanity of Human Wishes" (Bate, *Samuel Johnson* 282). The "inadequate or 'subjective' concept

exists apart from its perceptual content, or is manifest in the indistinctness or distortion of the empirical reality which it subsumes. Lacking in content, it is apprehended as an abstraction. *It is the truly abstract concept of which Johnson, as a mimetic theorist, disapproves.* . . . In mimetic writing the abstract or empty concept appears most often as unrealized convention" (Edinger 96).

11. Samuel Johnson, *The History of Rasselas, Prince of Abyssinia,* in *Rasselas and Other Tales,* vol. 14 of *The Yale Edition of the Works of Samuel Johnson,* ed. Gwin Kolb (New Haven: Yale UP, 1990), 163.

12. Samuel Johnson, *The Rambler,* No. 106, in vol. 4 of *The Yale Edition of the Works of Samuel Johnson,* ed. W. J. Bate and Albrecht B. Strauss (New Haven: Yale UP, 1969), 200. Henceforth, all *Rambler* citations will be from this edition. Each citation will give the essay, volume, and page number in parentheses; "R" will designate "*Rambler.*"

13. Walter Benjamin, "On Some Motifs in Baudelaire," in *Illuminations,* ed. Hannah Arendt, trans. Harry Zohn (New York: Schocken Books, 1969), 159.

14. Georg Lukács, *Studies in European Realism* (New York: Grosset and Dunlap, 1964), 91.

15. Max Horkheimer and Theodor Adorno, "The Culture Industry," in *Dialectic of Enlightenment,* trans. John Cumming (New York: Herder and Herder, 1972), 130.

16. *The Prelude 1799, 1805, 1850,* ed. Jonathan Wordsworth, M. H. Abrams, and Stephen Gill (New York: W. W. Norton, 1979; 1805), 258; 7.596–98.

17. Elias Canetti, *Crowds and Power,* trans. Carol Stewart (New York: Farrar, Straus and Giroux, 1984), 15–16.

18. " 'There is no private house, (said he,) in which people can enjoy themselves so well, as at a capital tavern.' " *Boswell's Life of Johnson,* ed. G. B. Hill (Oxford: Clarendon P, 1934), 2: 451. (Subsequent parenthetical references to this edition will cite it as "*Life.*") In a footnote Boswell quotes a passage from Hawkins's life of Johnson: "In contradiction to those, who, having a wife and children, prefer domestick enjoyments to those which a tavern affords, I have heard him assert, *that a tavern chair was the throne of human felicity.*—'As soon,' said he, 'as I enter the tavern, I experience an oblivion of care, and a freedom from solicitude: . . . wine exhilarates my spirits . . . : I dogmatise and am contradicted, and in this conflict of opinions and sentiments I find delight' " (2:452).

19. Richard Sennett, *The Fall of Public Man: On the Social Psychology of Capitalism* (New York: Vintage, 1978), 50.

20. On London crowds, see M. Dorothy George, *London Life in the Eighteenth Century* (Chicago: Academy Publishers, 1984), and Doro-

thy Marshall, *Dr. Johnson's London* (New York: John Wiley and Sons, 1968). The classic work on crowd behavior in the eighteenth century is George Rudé's *The Crowd in History, 1730–1848* (New York: John Wiley and Sons, 1964). E. P. Thompson discusses the ideological distortions in portraits of eighteenth-century crowd insurgency: see "The Moral Economy of the English Crowd in the Eighteenth Century," in *Customs in Common* (New York: New Press, 1991), 185–258. Rudé provides a useful overview of life in London in *Hanoverian London: 1714–1808* (Berkeley and Los Angeles: U of California P, 1971). See also Roy Porter, *English Society in the Eighteenth Century* (Harmondsworth: Penguin Books, 1990); and Richard B. Schwartz, *Daily Life in Johnson's London* (Madison: U of Wisconsin P, 1983). For discussions of the writer's place in eighteenth-century London, see Ian Watt, "Publishers and Sinners: The Augustan View," in *Studies in Bibliography,* ed. Fredson Bowers; Bibliographical Society of Virginia, vol. 12 (Charlottesville: U of Virginia P, 1959), 3–20; Terry Belanger, "Publishers and Writers in Eighteenth-Century England," in *Books and Their Readers in Eighteenth-Century England,* ed. Isabel Rivers (London: St. Martin's P, 1982), 5–25; and Alvin Kernan, *Samuel Johnson and the Impact of Print* (Princeton: Princeton UP, 1987).

21. "Preface to a Dictionary of the English Language," in *Samuel Johnson: Rasselas, Poems, and Selected Prose,* ed. Bertrand H. Bronson (3d ed.; New York: Holt, Rinehart, and Winston, 1971), 235.

22. For an extensive account of the *Dictionary's* moral aims, see Robert DeMaria Jr., *Johnson's Dictionary and the Language of Learning* (Chapel Hill: U of North Carolina P, 1986). DeMaria argues that Johnson's plan to use the illustrative quotations as a means of moral instruction had a tradition behind it. "Johnson uses philology for educational and therefore, of course, for moral purposes, but this particular way of combining linguistics and more fundamental goals was not at all new to lexicography" (13).

23. See John Bender's discussion of Defoe's meditation on symbolic attempts to ward off plague (*Imagining the Penitentiary: Fiction and the Architecture of Mind in Eighteenth-Century England* [Chicago: U of Chicago P, 1987], 73–84). Bender's general argument concerns one of the ways London regulated its citizens: it imposed itself on them as a metaphorical penitentiary. They learned to incorporate its authority in forms of internal surveillance, like prisoners in Bentham's panopticon.

24. See Max Byrd, *London Transformed: Images of the City in the Eighteenth Century* (New Haven: Yale UP, 1978). Byrd observes that the metaphor of the city as a human body is recurrent in eighteenth-century

literature, and helps contain in a coherent form its frightening distention (5, 31ff.).

25. Cf. William K. Wimsatt, *Philosophic Words: A Study of Style and Meaning in the "Rambler" and "Dictionary" of Samuel Johnson* (New Haven: Yale UP, 1948), 23–24.

26. Stanley Fish, "Commentary: The Young and the Restless," in *The New Historicism,* ed. H. Aram Veeser (New York: Routledge, 1989), 309.

1. The Desire for Fame

1. L. A. Selby-Bigge uses the term *sentimentalism* to characterize the social theories of Shaftesbury, Hutcheson, Butler, and Hume. "Introduction," *British Moralists, Being Selections from Writers Principally of the Eighteenth Century* (Indianapolis: Bobbs-Merrill, 1964).

2. Anthony, Earl of Shaftesbury, *Characteristics of Men, Manners, Opinions, Times, Etc.,* ed. John M. Robertson (London: Grant Richards, 1900), 1:75.

3. Adam Ferguson, *Essay on the History of Civil Society* (Boston: Hastings, Etheridge and Bliss, 1809), 362.

4. Bernard Mandeville, *The Fable of the Bees* (Harmondsworth: Penguin, 1989), 55.

5. David Hume, *A Treatise of Human Nature,* ed. L. A. Selby-Bigge (2d ed.; Oxford: Oxford UP, 1978), 534–39. For an account of Hume's notion of sympathy as a principle of social order, see John Mullan, *Sentiment and Sensibility* (Oxford: Clarendon P, 1988), 18–43.

6. See, for example, John Dunn, "From Applied Theology to Social Analysis: The Break between John Locke and the Scottish Enlightenment," in *Wealth and Virtue,* ed. Istvan Hunt and Michael Ignatieff (Cambridge: Cambridge UP, 1983), 119–36. Michael Ignatieff, *The Needs of Strangers* (New York: Viking Penguin, 1985), 81–103. Albert O. Hirschman, *The Passions and the Interests* (Princeton: Princeton UP, 1977), describes the drift of moral analysis of the passions toward economic analysis. See also J. G. A. Pocock, *The Machiavellian Moment: Florentine Political Thought and the Atlantic Republican Tradition* (Princeton: Princeton UP, 1975), and also by Pocock, *Virtue, Commerce, and History: Essays on Political Thought and History, Chiefly in the Eighteenth Century* (Cambridge: Cambridge UP, 1985).

7. John Barrell, *English Literature in History, 1730–80: An Equal, Wide Survey* (New York: St. Martin's, 1983), 30. I owe my Ferguson quotations to Barrell.

8. Adam Smith, *An Inquiry into the Nature and Causes of the Wealth of Nations,* ed. Edwin Cannan (Chicago: U of Chicago P, 1976), 2:303.

9. Thomas Carlyle describes Johnson's literary situation in similar though loftier terms. Johnson was a "hero," "one of our great English souls" (*On Heroes, Hero Worship and the Heroic in History,* ed. Carl Niemeyer [Lincoln: U of Nebraska P, 1966], 178), a believer in "the old formulas" during a "poor Paper-age, so barren, artificial, thick-quilted with Pedantries, Hearsays" (180). "That waste chaos in Authorship by Trade; that waste chaos of Scepticism in religion and politics, in life-theory and life-practice; in his poverty, in his dust and dimness, with the sick body and the rusty coat: he made it do for him, like a brave man" (184).

10. According to Robert Voitle, in *Samuel Johnson the Moralist* (Cambridge: Harvard UP, 1961), "Johnson opposed [the] whole tendency" of what Voitle calls the "school of Shaftesbury" (28). See also Nicholas Hudson, *Samuel Johnson and Eighteenth-Century Thought* (Oxford: Clarendon P, 1988), 61–64; and Leo Damrosch, *Fictions of Reality in the Age of Hume and Johnson* (Madison: U of Wisconsin P, 1989), 49.

11. Hester Piozzi, *Anecdotes of the Late Samuel Johnson,* in *Johnsonian Miscellanies,* vol. 1, ed. G. B. Hill (New York: Barnes and Noble, 1966), 268.

12. For more on Johnson and Mandeville, see Voitle (53–56), Hudson (129–36), and Earl Miner, "Dr. Johnson, Mandeville, and 'Publick Benefit,' " *HLQ* 21 (1958): 159–66.

13. Joseph Wood Krutch notes the relative rarity of "sociological" commentary in Johnson: *Rambler* No. 114, on prisons, is "one of the rather rare occasions when even he deals with what we should call a sociological rather than a moral subject" (39).

14. According to Paul Alkon, Johnson was so conscious of the massiveness and intractability of social machinery that he regarded social and political discussion generally a waste of time (21). Alkon draws the conclusion the present argument seeks to challenge or at least to complicate, that is, that Johnson hoped to affect social change through moral reflection. Alkon writes: "Measures imposed upon the mass of men from outside will all too often be smashed to bits against a coral roof built up of immovable individual dispositions. Therefore, the greatest hope for social improvement, he must have reasoned, rests in altering individual attitudes. . . . Consequently, Johnson's moral essays are his way of dealing with sociological issues" (22).

15. See Bate's account of the Mandevillean element of caricature in Johnson's character sketches (*Samuel Johnson,* 295).

16. Samuel Johnson, "Preface to Shakespeare," in *Johnson on Shakespeare,* vol. 7 of *The Yale Edition of the Works of Samuel Johnson,* ed. Arthur Sherbo (New Haven: Yale UP, 1968), 61.

17. See Hoyt Trowbridge, "Scattered Atoms of Probability," *Eighteenth-Century Studies* 5:1 (1971): 1–38.
18. Cf. Alkon, who observes that *Rambler* No. 146 depicts the "struggle against the uncomfortable feeling of being lost in the crowd. Almost anything is preferable to that" (137).
19. Alvin Kernan argues that the impersonality of print culture drove Johnson to lay special emphasis on forms of personal uniqueness, either in the text or the author's character. This was part of a general cultural trend "to, as we would now say, remystify or privilege the literary text, or in Benjamin's terms to provide these printed literary works with an aura" (157). Johnson shows how "letters in general . . . created over time an aura for its printed texts" (158). He did it in part by insisting on his personal peculiarity. Leo Braudy, in *The Frenzy of Renown: Fame and Its History* (Oxford: Oxford UP, 1988), discusses Boswell's fascination with celebrity, which, Braudy argues, responds to the "vacuum of cultural authority" at a time when public life exclusively defined honor and fame (371). "The attack on external authority had resulted in a confusion over what a valid authority was. . . . Into that gap of authority stepped those warlocks of individualism, the wise men of the eighteenth century" (371).
20. Sennett, *The Fall of Public Man*, 64–88.
21. T. F. Wharton argues (in *Samuel Johnson and the Theme of Hope* [London: Macmillan, 1984]) that Johnson's anger at high society's neglect of authors (71) drove him to seek isolation by way of retaliation: "Isolation is in fact willingly embraced" (72).
22. Voitle praises Johnson's charity (119) and reminds us that Hawkins, who puzzled over Johnson's household, nevertheless compared him to Thomas à Kempis (122). William Hazlitt was moved to think of him "carrying the unfortunate victim of disease and dissipation on his back up through Fleet Street, (an act which realises the parable of the good Samaritan)" (*Lectures on the English Comic Writers* [London: J. M. Dent, 1963], 103–4). John Wain writes in *Samuel Johnson* (New York: Viking, 1974) that Johnson might aptly "be called one of the most benevolent men who ever lived" (267). The "opulence and comfort of his surroundings at the Thrales never caused him to forget that the mass of humanity lived in sweat and poverty. Always Johnson kept the poor and the unfortunate in his thoughts" (266).
23. Lyle Larsen, *Dr. Johnson's Household* (Hamden, Conn.: Archon Books, 1985), 48.
24. James Boswell, *Boswell in Extremes: 1776–1778,* ed. Charles McC. Weis and Frederick A. Pottle (New York: McGraw-Hill, 1970), 301. I owe the citations from Boswell to Larsen (44, 57, 72).

25. Johnson credits Addison and Steele with the introduction of domestic life into English literature. "Before the *Tatler* and *Spectator,* if the writers for the theatre are excepted, England had no masters of common life. No writers had yet undertaken to reform either the savageness of neglect, or the impertinence of civility" (*Lives of the English Poets,* ed. G. B. Hill [Oxford: Clarendon P, 1905], 2:93). They turned to commentary on domestic manners as a way of staying out of political strife. Such topics tended "to divert the attention of the people from publick discontent" (2:94). To "minds heated with political contest, [The *Tatler* and *Spectator*] supplied cooler and more inoffensive reflections" (2:94). They courted "general approbation by general topics, and subjects on which faction had produced no diversity of sentiments, such as literature, morality, and familiar life" (2:92). It was for this reason that Pope was able likewise to converse "indifferently with both parties, and never disturbed the publick with political opinions" (*Lives* 3:109).

    Walter Benjamin notes, similarly, the apolitical character of the *feuilleton,* which became popular in Paris in the nineteenth century. Since this portion of the newspaper depended on advertisers and could not afford to antagonize them, it steered clear of critical social commentary and politics, and entertained the reader instead with "[c]ity gossip, theatrical intrigues, and 'things worth knowing' " ("The Paris of the Second Empire in Baudelaire," in *Charles Baudelaire: A Lyric Poet in the Era of High Capitalism,* trans. Harry Zohn [London: Verso, 1983], 28). In the character sketches or "physiologies" that enjoyed a vogue in these pages, "[i]nnocuousness was of the essence" (36).

26. Voitle suggests (108–9) that Johnson approved of Richard Cumberland's scheme in *The Laws of Nature* for reconciling individuals and social order as a whole. This is the role of social subordination, which organizes humans like particles in order to build "this most beautiful *Frame* of the Material *World*" (109). Laboring at one's modest task is beneficial to others even if one does not see or know them. But Voitle implies later that this conception of social service may not work in a crowd: "That [the argument in *Rambler* No. 99] which is so telling against universal benevolence can be used against the effectiveness of the altruistic motive in the nation, the unit with which his social, political, and economic observations are usually concerned, Johnson would be the last to deny. We have already seen that most men are necessarily limited to the sort of indirect benevolence which results from labouring at one's task. This is why there is so little systematic discussion of political and social theory in his works" (117). Despite

the talk of subordination and Cumberland, Voitle agrees that the problem of the crowd disjoins moral from political speculation.

27. Alkon explains that manuals for Anglican ministers formalized the mode of the sermon. He quotes John Wilkins's *Ecclesiastes: or A Discourse Concerning the Gift of Preaching, As It Falls under the Rules of Art* (6th ed.; London, 1679), 6–7. The manual defines method as "an Art of contriving our discourse in such regular frame, wherein every part may have its due place and dependence"; the method "which our gravest Divines by long experience have found most useful for ordinary and populous Assemblies, is this of *Doctrine* and *Use*" (Alkon 184). See also James Gray, *Johnson's Sermons: A Study* (Oxford: Clarendon P, 1972): "Both in his choice of theme and in the manner of his presentation of them, Johnson clearly belongs to the Puritan homiletical tradition" (124). Johnson preferred the style of "the seventeenth-century divines who . . . practised a plain, direct, unadorned expression of theological truths" (125). Gray cites the example of Samuel D'Oyley, *Christian Eloquence in Theory and Practice* (1722), who recommends solid argument, orderly disposition, well-chosen citation, elevated expression, and novel thought, but rejects ornament (127).

28. W. J. Bate cites this essay as an example of "satire *manqué*" (496), the form of compassionate humor he argues that Johnson adopted instead of the satirical humor that came to him naturally. Johnson identified with the objects of his incipient satire and so refrained from attack. In *Rambler* No. 146, though, the humor does not involve compassionate identification, but rather an apprehension of the insignificance of persons. Bate is right that Johnson declines satire here; he does so, though, not because his target deserves sympathy, but because satire is too personal. The target is *beneath* satire.

2. Periodical Moralizing

1. Richard Holmes, *Dr. Johnson and Mr. Savage* (London: Hodder and Stoughton, 1993), 45.

2. Samuel Johnson, *Adventurer*, No. 115, in vol. 2 of *The Yale Edition of the Works of Samuel Johnson*, ed. W. J. Bate, J. M. Bullitt, and L. F. Powell (New Haven: Yale UP, 1963), 457. Henceforth all *Adventurer* and *Idler* citations will be from this edition. Each citation will give the essay, volume, and page number in parentheses; "A" will designate "*Adventurer*" and "I" will designate "*Idler*."

3. Paul Fussell, *Samuel Johnson and the Life of Writing* (New York: Harcourt, Brace, Jovanovich, 1971), 156ff.

4. Samuel Johnson, *Diaries, Prayers, and Annals*, in vol. 1 of *The Yale*

Edition of the Works of Samuel Johnson, ed. E. L. McAdam Jr. and Donald and Mary Hyde (New Haven: Yale UP, 1958), 73.

5. Alkon points out Johnson's opposition to "ruling passion" theory (in *Pope*) by way of insisting on the primacy of intellectual freedom in moral action (25–26). Voitle makes the same point (25).

6. According to Sachs, Johnson opposed "bad particularity"; in contrast to it, he imagines "another kind . . . that is positive and is in fact the essence of Reason's work. The general arises from moving flexibly handled particulars that are reasoned into law and principle" (87). This is the view I am especially opposing. For a contrasting view of particularity, see Deidre Lynch, " 'Beating the Track of the Alphabet': Samuel Johnson, Tourism, and the ABCs of Modern Authority," *ELH* 57 (1990): 357–405. This article attacks the habit of distinguishing between Johnson as a scholar and as a man of the world, and argues that Johnson's sense of the "experiential" and "particular" is intrinsically literary and ideological. My own distinction between the scholar's closet and the "world" may seem to lie open to Lynch's criticism. It is important to stress, therefore, that the "crowd" is figurative in Johnson; it overflows the boundary between the domains of life and literature.

7. On maxims, see Isobel Grundy, "Samuel Johnson: Man of Maxims?" Bate discusses the compression of Johnson's sentences in *Samuel Johnson,* 282.

8. Alkon observes that Johnson's concept of "artificial passions" in addition to six "primary passions" (14–15) allows "for rich variety without losing sight of a comforting thread of underlying uniformity" (37).

9. Alkon argues that, for Johnson, pity (culminating in charity) is unique among the passions in that it is the only one that cannot be explained according to the dictates of self-interest or natural necessity. It has to be learned: children do not feel pity, according to Johnson. Its unnaturalness is a token of its divine origin (39–43). John Dussinger makes a similar argument for pity in his account of the *Life of Savage,* "Dr. Johnson's Solemn Response to Beneficence," in *Domestic Privacies: Samuel Johnson and the Art of Biography,* ed. David Wheeler (Lexington: University Press of Kentucky, 1987), 57–69.

10. Sachs concludes from *Rasselas,* chapter 28, that "we differ . . . when we see only part . . . but when we perceive the whole at once, all agree in one judgement" (77); and from chapter 11: "We grow more happy as our minds take a wider range."

11. See R 188, R 206, I 83; and related essays, I 57 and I 100.

12. T. F. Wharton makes this point (70–72), citing R 2, 40, 87, 144, and 183.

13. Wharton argues, against Boswell, that Johnson wrote *Rasselas* not after but during his mother's death, perhaps as an excuse not to attend her (91–92). If Wharton is right, *Rasselas* might be expected to express a kind of defiance of mourning rituals, and at the same time, perhaps, some sense of guilt. Wharton suggests that Johnson's diffidence about ritual appears in his portrait of Nekayah when she mourns Pekuah's loss.

14. See Edward Tomarken, *Johnson, Rasselas, and the Choice of Criticism* (Lexington: University Press of Kentucky, 1989), which argues that the conversational setting of *Rasselas* transforms the characters' Johnsonian generalizations. Instead of authoritative statements about life, they appear as relative positions taken under the pressure of the moment.

15. Tomarken suggests that Johnson refrains from drowning the inventor by way of suggesting that technological experience is cumulative: the inventor will do better next time (49–51). By implication, moral wisdom is cumulative, too. But the inventor's survival does not suggest accumulation of perspective: his wings help him float in the water, but he will not make use of this property next time (not even as a "backup"). The passage is framed to highlight the contrast between lofty imagining and material circumstance. Instead of accumulation of perspective, the passage suggests that the useless perspective of moral contemplation helps one withstand disappointment, but that it is jury-rigged and absurdly cumbersome.

16. Franz Kafka imagined after writing "The Judgment" that writing would be a solace and a salvation. Maurice Blanchot, in "Kafka et l'exigence de l'oeuvre," *L'espace litteraire* (Paris: Gallimard, 1955), 59–98, describes Kafka's increasing estrangement from his work as the years passed. It became less and less clear to him why he was writing, though the pressure to write remained exigent. Johnson evokes imagination as this sort of compulsion in the scene at the pyramids.

3. The Vanity of Human Wishes

1. See D. V. Boyd, "Vanity and Vacuity: A Reading of Johnson's Verse Satires," *ELH* 39: 3 (1972): 387–403; Bate, *Samuel Johnson*, 282; Mary Lascelles, "Johnson and Juvenal," in *New Light on Dr. Johnson*, ed. F. W. Hilles (New Haven: Yale UP, 1959), 35–55; Damrosch, *Samuel Johnson and the Tragic Sense*, 139–59; Patrick O'Flaherty, "Johnson as Satirist: A New Look at *The Vanity of Human Wishes*," *ELH* 34 (1967): 78–91. Some critics have argued, conversely, that the poem is predominantly satirical and that it blocks sympathetic identification with

the characters. See Howard D. Weinbrot, *The Formal Strain* (Chicago: U of Chicago P, 1969), 193–217, which argues that Johnson means to ridicule the vain endeavor of worldly striving and to praise the calm that comes from celestial wisdom (217). See also Donald Greene, "On Misreading Eighteenth-Century Literature: A Rejoinder," *Eighteenth-Century Studies* 9 (1976): 108–18, which attacks Damrosch and argues that the poem's "victims of perverted values" are "farcical, not tragic" figures. Wharton and Vesterman, like Boyd, rise appealingly above this fray: they accept the grim (if not tragic) reading of the poem while attending to the impersonality of its rhetoric.

2. In the *Life of Pope* Johnson writes that imitation "pleases when the thoughts are unexpectedly applicable and the parallels lucky" (3:176). He notes that imitation is difficult: a learned reader "will . . . often detect strained applications . . . [and] the work will be generally uncouth and party-coloured" (3:247). For an account of the fashion of literary imitation, see Weinbrot, 1–30, and Lascelles, 38.

3. The debate about the poem's tone—whether tragic or satirical—is fueled by the ambiguity of its style of exemplification. Greene and Weinbrot find the portraits deliberately shallow and narrow; Damrosch, by contrast, speaks of Johnson "transforming passages of vivid . . . particularity into something much more solemn and general" (148). Wharton praises Johnson's talent for compressing a general pattern into tiny details (like the detail of Xerxes' encumbered oar) (48–49). "Nearly all the coarse elements of Juvenal's derision are stripped away. . . . In their place comes a humane comprehension of human needs and human mechanisms" (51). Bate writes that the poem's lines on the statesman "are typical of Johnson because they give the abstract generalization and also pin it at once to concrete human behavior" (*Samuel Johnson* 285).

4. Both Damrosch (154) and Bate (*Samuel Johnson* 279, 281) stress the connection between the poem and Ecclesiastes.

5. "The Vanity of Human Wishes," *Poems,* in vol. 6 of *The Yale Edition of the Works of Samuel Johnson,* ed. E. L. McAdam Jr. and George Milne (New Haven: Yale UP, 1964), 11. 15–16.

6. I disagree here with Vesterman and Bate. Vesterman: "the very qualities that define a self are those that cause its destruction" (116); and [j]ust as Wolsey's motive has been his defeat, his wish itself is the reason for its failure" (117). Bate: "In the alchemy of man's nature as it interacts with his world, each wish . . . and each 'gift of nature' and 'grace of art' become sources of disaster. Because the betrayal is from within, the human being seems peculiarly defenseless before it" (*Samuel Johnson* 282). Vesterman and Bate see desire as the "source" of

affliction; but Johnson suggests that misery is impersonal and that desire is added onto it.

7. See "The Concrete Universal" (69–83) and "The Structure of Romantic Nature Imagery" (103–16) in *The Verbal Icon: Studies in the Meaning of Poetry* (Lexington: University Press of Kentucky, 1954). The classic critique of Wimsatt's reading of romantic symbolism is Paul de Man's "The Rhetoric of Temporality," in *Blindness and Insight: Essay in the Rhetoric of Contemporary Criticism* (2d ed.; Minneapolis: U of Minnesota P, 1983), 187–228. In de Man's terms, Johnson may be seen as renouncing the "symbol" in favor of "allegory." He thematizes the figurative nature of the reconciliation of the general and the particular.

8. In *Samuel Johnson after Deconstruction* (Carbondale: Southern Illinois UP, 1992) Steven Lynn points out Johnson's use of the word "supplemental" in *Rambler* No. 41: "So few of the hours of life are filled up with objects adequate to the mind of man, and so frequently are we in want of present pleasure or employment, that we are forced to have recourse to the past and future for supplemental satisfactions" (3:221). Lynn: "Johnson's reference here to 'supplemental satisfactions' would seem to exemplify Derrida's important concept of the unavoidable 'supplement' " (75). On "supplementarity," see Jacques Derrida, *Of Grammatology,* trans. Gayatri Spivak (Baltimore: Johns Hopkins UP, 1976), 141–64. Johnson, of course, despised Rousseau.

9. Boyd notices this effect: "[T]he tragic wheel of Fortune takes a special twist in Johnson's hands: 'Delusive Fortune hears th'incessant call / They mount, they shine, evaporate, and fall" (75–76). The sequence of rise, triumph, and fall is what we conventionally expect of tragedy, but it is the element of 'evaporation' that distinguishes Johnson's vision. . . . This process is clearest in the portrait of Wolsey. The conventionally tragic external fall is actually anticlimactic, being preceded by a psychological fall of greater import" (397).

10. Damrosch speaks of the "disparity between Juvenal's Hannibal" and Johnson's Charles, a much more dignified figure (143). Weinbrot disagrees that there is much gain in dignity, let alone tragic greatness: Charles is pathetic and misguided, but not tragic (204–6). Weinbrot seems right in saying that the passage is abrupt and dismissive, but Damrosch is right, conversely, in insisting that the passage is profoundly grim.

11. Juvenal, "Satire X," *Juvenal and Persius,* trans. G. G. Ramsay, (Cambridge: Harvard UP, 1918), 201.

12. "When Dr. Johnson read his own satire . . . he burst into a passion of tears one day" (Piozzi 180).

13. Bate talks about the crowds in the poem (*Achievement* 19).

14. Ian Jack, in *Augustan Satire: Intention and Idiom in English Poetry, 1660–1750* (Oxford: Clarendon P, 1957), calls "the" in Johnson's usage the "generic article" (142). Johnson "felt this to be a gain in elevation and in philosophical generality, though not in conciseness" (142).

4. Exemplary Self-Sacrifice

1. Johnson, *An Account of the Life of Mr. Richard Savage,* ed. Clarence Tracy (Oxford: Clarendon P, 1971), 13.

2. Critics have noted that she seems unreal, like a wicked stepmother in a fairy tale. See Isobel Grundy, *Samuel Johnson and the Scale of Greatness* (Athens: U of Georgia P, 1986), 139; John Dussinger, "Style and Intention in Johnson's *Life of Savage,*" *ELH* 37 (1970): 564–80; and William Vesterman, "Johnson and *The Life of Savage,*" *ELH* 36 (1969): 659–78.

3. For an account of the conflict in the *Life* between the Christian topic of charity and the corrupt patronage system, see Dussinger, "Dr. Johnson's Solemn Response to Beneficence," 57–69.

4. Some critics regard Johnson's ambivalence as a product of his powers of sympathy. See Dussinger, "Dr. Johnson's Solemn Response to Beneficence"; also Michael M. Cohen, "The Enchained Heart and the Puzzled Biographer: Johnson's *Life of Savage,*" *The New Rambler: Journal of the Johnson Society of London* 18 (1977): 33–40; and Martin Maner, "Satire and Sympathy in Johnson's *Life of Savage,*" *Genre* 8 (1975): 107–18. To some extent, though, Savage's story is about trying to live without sympathy—to meet the impersonality of the city on its own cold terms; that is the effort I think Johnson wants to come to terms with and feels ambivalent about. In "Johnson and *The Life of Savage*" William Vesterman argues—more persuasively, I think, than the aforementioned authors—that Johnson is ambivalent because he wants to distance himself from a melodramatic rhetoric of morality which he associates with both Savage and his enemies. For an elaboration of this idea in psychoanalytic terms, see Fredric Bogel, "Johnson and the Role of Authority," in *The New 18th Century,* ed. Felicity Nussbaum and Laura Brown (New York: Methuen, 1987), 189–209.

5. Tracy notes that Johnson wrote "Added" in the margin opposite the sentence beginning "This Relation will not be wholly without its Use. . . . " Presumably Johnson felt his remark about wise men might be mistaken as a license for lax behavior. He therefore *added* the moral reminder. The move from Savage's "condition" to its moral sense is consistently this one of supplementary addition. For more on the conflict between the two sentences, see Vesterman (659–60) and Bogel (197–98).

6. See "Style and Intention in Johnson's *Life of Savage*," 569.

7. As, for example, Cohen argues in "The Enchained Heart and the Puzzled Biographer," 37.

8. Barry Cunliffe, *The City of Bath* (New Haven: Yale UP, 1986), 54, 100–102, 112–45. Cunliffe writes: "to maintain its allure for the idle rich Bath had to become a gambling town of elegance, more a Monaco than a Las Vegas" (114). Interestingly, Johnson notes that, when Savage was imprisoned at Newgate, "Beau" Nash, the impresario behind Bath's transformation, sent Savage five guineas, and promised to promote his subscription at Bath (124).

9. See Holmes, 75–78; also Clarence Tracy, *The Artificial Bastard: A Biography of Richard Savage* (Cambridge: Cambridge UP, 1953), 60ff.

10. Bogel, "Johnson and the Role of Authority," 195.

11. In the "Preface" to *Shakespeare*, Johnson warns against details that depict merely "adventitious peculiarities of personal habits"; they are like "superficial dies, bright and pleasing for a little while, yet soon fading to a dim tinct" (70). Commenting on this passage in *Samuel Johnson and Poetic Style*, William Edinger argues that it illustrates Johnson's preference for a quasi-Hegelian or Lukácsian representational style, which Edinger, recalling Wimsatt, calls "concrete universality" (83–92). But part of the moral of *Rambler* No. 60 and of the *Life of Savage* is, I think, that only an idealized or merely theoretical "concrete universality" is available to writers like Savage and Johnson: there is no "organic" relation between them and the public world. Johnson believes, rather, that the public world imposes "exterior appendages" on them, and that actions become morally legible only among "domestick privacies."

12. Cf. Toni O'Shaughnessy, "Fiction as Truth: Personal Identity in Johnson's *Life of Savage*," *Studies in English Literature* 30 (1990): 487–501. More than most other treatments, this article attends to the connection, in the *Life*, between rhetoric and the self. At times, though, it loses sight of the material dimension of Johnson's rhetorical equation; for O'Shaughnessy, rhetoric—and with it the self—come simply to mean "fiction."

13. There is a distinct rhetorical equivalent, in eighteenth-century biography, to the union of precept and example: that is, the section of the biography called the "character." As a separate genre, the "character" has a long history; critics number Pausanius, Plutarch, and Sallust among Johnson's ancient precursors. On the "character," see Folkenflik (100–101); Cohen (34); Lawrence Lipking, *The Ordering of the Arts in Eighteenth-Century England* (Princeton: Princeton UP, 1970), 420–22, 446–53; and Jean Hagstrum, *Samuel Johnson's Literary Criticism*, 38–41. For a general account of Johnson's place in the history of

biography in England, see Donald Stauffer, *The Art of Biography in Eighteenth-Century England* (Princeton: Princeton UP, 1941), 386–402.

14. This is the notion of character that William Hazlitt, a generation after Johnson, will particularly deplore. For him, "personal character" consists precisely in its "whims and humours"; it is not a "machine or collection of topics" (*The Spirit of the Age* [New York: Dent and Dutton, 1967], 299).

15. See *Idler* No. 3, as well.

16. The paragraph concerning *On Public Works* goes on to scorn the idea of colonization as a solution to political problems. See Greene's discussion of the passage in *The Politics of Samuel Johnson* (New Haven: Yale UP, 1960), 135–37.

17. Dussinger, "Style and Intention in Johnson's *Life of Savage*," 579.

18. See Robert Folkenflik, *Samuel Johnson, Biographer* on the role of "peculiarities" in *Pope, Addison,* and the "Life of Browne" (40–41).

   Peculiarity of character distinguishes a character by its oddity. "I will add one or two peculiarities more, before I lay down my pen," writes Hester Piozzi at the end of her *Anecdotes;* then she tells how Johnson, though so uncouth in form and figure himself, "did not like another man much the less for being a coxcomb" (348–49); and how, though a man of obscure birth, he showed his "partiality to people of family . . . on every occasion" (349). Anna Howe offers the sort of apology that seems inherent in such accounts of temperamental oddity: "Don't chide me one bit for [my wicked liveliness], my dear. It is nature. I can't help it. Nay, for that matter, I love it, and wish not to help it. So spare your gravity, I beseech you on this subject. I set up not for a perfect character" (Samuel Richardson, *Clarissa* [New York: Dent and Dutton, 1967], 1:333).

19. Bogel, "Johnson and the Role of Authority," 196.

20. Dussinger summarizes this motif succinctly in "Style and Intention in Johnson's *Life of Savage*," 579.

21. In *Adventurer* No. 131, Johnson speaks of "singularity" as a "spot" on a "character." "Men of this kind [who consign themselves to singularity] are generally known by the name of humourists, an appellation by which he that has obtained it, and can be contented to keep it, is set free at once from the shackles of fashion; and can go in or out, sit or stand, be talkative or silent, gloomy or merry, advance absurdities or oppose demonstration, without any other reprehension from mankind, than that it is his way, that he is an odd fellow, and must be let alone. . . . These peculiarities, however, are always found to spot a character though they may not totally obscure it; and he who expects

from mankind, that they should give up established customs in compliance with his single will, and exacts that deference which he does not pay, may be endured, but can never be approved" (2:484–85).

22. Benjamin, "Some Motifs in Baudelaire," 171. In *The Rise of the Novel* (Berkeley and Los Angeles: U of California P, 1957), Ian Watt observes how Defoe attends to the weight and density of objects in a scene where Moll Flanders tries to steal a woman's watch in a crowd. The scene has a "practical moral" but it also appeals to the reader as mass of details; yet the scene's vividness is "curiously incidental" (97). Like Johnson and Poe, Defoe evokes the disassembly of details in a crowd, their decay into morally insignificant materiality.

23. Dussinger, "Style and Intention in Johnson's *Life of Savage*," 568.

24. For a discussion of carnivals and the grotesque in the middle ages, and their displacement and suppression in the eighteenth century, see Peter Stallybrass and Allon White, *The Politics and Poetics of Transgression* (Ithaca: Cornell UP, 1986). This is a good account of a tradition Savage flirts with but utterly fails to represent.

5. Probability and Conjecture

1. For a good history of the rise of probability theory in the seventeenth and eighteenth centuries, see Ian Hacking, *The Emergence of Probability: A Philosophical Study of Early Ideas about Probability, Induction, and Statistical Inference* (London: Cambridge UP, 1975). For a treatment of literary interest in the idea of probability, see Douglas Lane Patey, *Probability and Literary Form: Philosophic Theory and Literary Practice in the Augustan Age* (Cambridge: Cambridge UP, 1984). The key work on Johnson and probability remains Hoyt Trowbridge, "Scattered Atoms of Probability." See also Damrosch, *Fictions of Reality in the Age of Hume and Johnson,* 42–48.

2. Benjamin, "Some Motifs in Baudelaire," 115.

3. Benedict Anderson, *Imagined Communities: Reflections on the Origin and Spread of Nationalism* (London: Verso, 1983), 30.

4. "A fallible being will fail somewhere," he said to Boswell (*Life* 2:132).

5. Lukács, *Studies in European Realism,* 91, 147ff.

Conclusion

1. Jean-François Lyotard, *Just Gaming,* trans. Wlad Godzich (Minneapolis: U of Minnesota P, 1985).

2. Greene, *The Politics of Samuel Johnson,* 253.

3. "The False Alarm," *Political Writings,* vol. 10 of *The Yale Edition of the Works of Samuel Johnson,* ed. Donald Greene (New Haven: Yale UP,

1977), 328. All subsequent citations from Johnson's political writings will come from this edition.

4. "Thoughts on the Late Transactions Respecting Falkland's Islands. 1771," *Political Writings,* 366.

5. "Preface" to the *Dictionary,* 238.

6. See Leo Damrosch, *Fictions of Reality in the Age of Hume and Johnson.*

7. Leo Damrosch, in *Fictions of Reality in the Age of Hume and Johnson,* explains brilliantly that Johnson's conservatism arose from his skeptical sense that social order depended predominantly on an arbitrary consensus. In Johnson's view, the "consensus of the group simply *is* the way the world makes sense, and it is not 'just' because there is no transcendental standard from which to reject that standard" (18). Johnson had a "deep emotional commitment" to social subordination (53) because it assured the sense-making condition of public consensus. His "conservativism . . . expresses the unease of a culture that venerates its past but is increasingly immersed in rapid and irreversible change. . . . What is at stake, very clearly, is an incipient breakdown of consensus" (56–57).

8. Johnson says in Boswell's *Life:* "[M]ankind are happier in a state of inequality and subordination. Were they to be in this pretty state of equality, they would soon degenerate into brutes. . . . Sir, all would be losers were all to work for all:—they would have no intellectual improvement. All intellectual improvement arises from leisure; all leisure arises from one working for another" (2:219).

9. See Peter Linebaugh, *The London Hanged: Crime and Civil Society in the Eighteenth Century* (Cambridge: Cambridge UP, 1992). Linebaugh argues that London's proletariat in the eighteenth century survived only by forms of pilfering loosely sanctioned by custom. They lived on a borderline of illegality that Johnson must have found intolerable. "Regulating" them required greater rationalization of the penal code and eventually the application of coercive bureaucratic principles to the workplace.

10. "Taxation No Tyranny," *Political Writings,* 454.

11. These are Greene's illustrations (180).

12. Albert Hirschman, *The Rhetoric of Reaction: Perversity, Futility, Jeopardy* (Cambridge: Belknap P, 1991).

13. Greene summarizes the situation efficiently (205). See also George Rudé, *Wilkes and Liberty* (Oxford: Clarendon P, 1962).

14. Addison, *The Spectator,* No. 413 (London: J. M. Dent and Sons, 1945), 3:283.

15. Deirdre Bair writes in *Samuel Beckett* (New York: Harcourt Brace Jovanovich, 1977) that Beckett "still reads" Johnson. "He finds much

that appeals to him, particularly the melancholy moods and depressions which characterized Johnson's later life: 'there can hardly have been many so completely at sea in their solitude as he was or so horribly aware of it. Read the Prayers and Meditations if you don't believe me' " (256).

16. For a thoughtful account of politics and imagination in the *Journey to the Western Islands of Scotland,* see Alison Hickey, " 'Extensive Views' in Johnson's *Journey to the Western Islands of Scotland,*" *Studies in English Literature* 32:3 (1992): 537–53.

Works Cited

Addison, Joseph. *The Spectator.* 4 vols. London: J. M. Dent and Sons, 1945.

Alkon, Paul. *Samuel Johnson and Moral Discipline.* Evanston: Northwestern UP, 1969.

Anderson, Benedict. *Imagined Communities: Reflections on the Origin and Spread of Nationalism.* London: Verso, 1983.

Bair, Deirdre. *Samuel Beckett.* New York: Harcourt, Brace, and Jovanovich, 1977.

Barrell, John. *English Literature in History, 1730–80: An Equal, Wide Survey.* New York: St. Martin's, 1983.

Bate, W. J. *Samuel Johnson.* New York: Harcourt, Brace, and Jovanovich, 1976.

——. *The Achievement of Samuel Johnson.* New York: Oxford UP, 1955.

Belanger, Terry. "Publishers and Writers in Eighteenth-Century England." *Books and Their Readers in Eighteenth-Century England.* Ed. Isabel Rivers. London: St. Martin's, 1982. 5–25.

Bender, John. *Imagining the Penitentiary: Fiction and the Architecture of Mind in Eighteenth-Century England.* Chicago: U of Chicago P, 1987.

Benjamin, Walter. "On Some Motifs in Baudelaire." In *Illuminations.* Ed. Hannah Arendt. Trans. Harry Zohn. New York: Schocken Books, 1969. 155–200.

——. "The Paris of the Second Empire in Baudelaire." *Charles Baudelaire: A Lyric Poet in the Era of High Capitalism.* Trans. Harry Zohn. London: Verso, 1983. 11–106.

Blanchot, Maurice. "Kafka et l'exigence de l'oeuvre." In *L'espace littéraire.* Paris: Gallimard, 1955. 59–98.

Bogel, Fredric. "Johnson and the Role of Authority." *The New Eighteenth Century.* Ed. Felicity Nussbaum and Laura Brown. New York: Methuen, 1987. 189–209.

Boswell, James. *Boswell in Extremes: 1776–1778.* Ed. Charles McC. Weis and Frederick A. Pottle. New York: McGraw-Hill, 1970.

——. *Boswell's Life of Johnson.* 4 vols. Ed. G. B. Hill. Oxford: Clarendon P, 1934.

Boyd, D. V. "Vanity and Vacuity: A Reading of Johnson's Verse Satires." *ELH* 39 (1972): 387–403.

Braudy, Leo. *The Frenzy of Renown: Fame and Its History.* Oxford: Oxford UP, 1988.

Bronson, Bertrand. "Johnson Agonistes." In *Johnson Agonistes and Other Essays.* Cambridge: Cambridge UP, 1946. 1–52.

Byrd, Max. *London Transformed: Images of the City in the Eighteenth Century.* New Haven: Yale UP, 1978.

Canetti, Elias. *Crowds and Power.* Trans. Carol Stewart. New York: Farrar, Straus and Giroux, 1984.

Carlyle, Thomas. *On Heroes, Hero Worship and the Heroic in History.* Ed. Carl Niemeyer. Lincoln: U of Nebraska P, 1966.

Cohen, Michael M. "The Enchained Heart and the Puzzled Biographer: Johnson's *Life of Savage.*" *The New Rambler: Journal of the Johnson Society of London* 18 (1977): 33–40.

Cunliffe, Barry. *The City of Bath.* New Haven: Yale UP, 1986.

Damrosch, Leo. *Fictions of Reality in the Age of Hume and Johnson.* Madison: U of Wisconsin P, 1989.

——. *Samuel Johnson and the Tragic Sense.* Princeton: Princeton UP, 1972.

Davis, Philip. *In Mind of Johnson: A Study of Johnson the Rambler.* Athens: U of Georgia P, 1989.

de Man, Paul. "The Rhetoric of Temporality." In *Blindness and Insight: Essays in the Rhetoric of Contemporary Criticism.* 2d ed. Minneapolis: U of Minnesota P, 1983. 187–228.

DeMaria, Robert, Jr. *Johnson's Dictionary and the Language of Learning.* Chapel Hill: U of North Carolina P, 1986.

Derrida, Jacques. *Of Grammatology.* Trans. Gayatri Spivak. Baltimore: Johns Hopkins UP, 1976.

Dunn, John. "From Applied Theology to Social Analysis: The Break between John Locke and the Scottish Enlightenment." *Wealth and Virtue.* Ed. Istvan Hunt and Michael Ignatieff. Cambridge: Cambridge UP, 1983. 119–36.

Dussinger, John. "Dr. Johnson's Solemn Response to Beneficence." *Domestic Privacies: Samuel Johnson and the Art of Biography.* Ed. David Wheeler. Lexington: University Press of Kentucky, 1987. 57–69.

——. "Style and Intention in Johnson's *Life of Savage.*" *ELH* 37 (1970): 564–80.

Edinger, William. *Samuel Johnson and Poetic Style.* Chicago: U of Chicago P, 1977.

Ferguson, Adam. *Essay on the History of Civil Society.* Boston: Hastings, Etheridge and Bliss, 1809.

Fish, Stanley. "Commentary: The Young and the Restless." *The New Historicism.* Ed. H. Aram Veeser. New York: Routledge, 1989. 303–16.

Folkenflik, Robert. *Samuel Johnson, Biographer.* Ithaca: Cornell UP, 1978.

Fussell, Paul. *Samuel Johnson and the Life of Writing*. New York: Harcourt, Brace, Jovanovich, 1971.

George, M. Dorothy. *London Life in the Eighteenth Century*. Chicago: Academy Publishers, 1984.

Gray, James. *Johnson's Sermons: A Study*. Oxford: Clarendon P, 1972.

Greene, Donald. "On Misreading Eighteenth-Century Literature: A Rejoinder." *Eighteenth-Century Studies* 9 (1976): 108–18.

——. *The Politics of Samuel Johnson*. New Haven: Yale UP, 1960.

Grundy, Isobel. "Samuel Johnson: Man of Maxims?" *Samuel Johnson: New Critical Essays*. Ed. Isobel Grundy. London: Vision P, 1984. 13–30.

——. *Samuel Johnson and the Scale of Greatness*. Athens: U of Georgia P, 1986.

Hacking, Ian. *The Emergence of Probability: A Philosophical Study of Early Ideas about Probability, Induction, and Statistical Inference*. London: Cambridge UP, 1975.

Hagstrum, Jean. *Samuel Johnson's Literary Criticism*. Minneapolis: U of Minneapolis P, 1952.

Hazlitt, William. *Lectures on the English Comic Writers*. London: J. M. Dent, 1963.

——. *The Spirit of the Age*. New York: Dent and Dutton, 1967.

Hickey, Alison. " 'Extensive Views' in Johnson's *Journey to the Western Islands of Scotland*." *Studies in English Literature* 32 (1992): 537–53.

Hirschman, Albert O. *The Passions and the Interests*. Princeton: Princeton UP, 1977.

——. *The Rhetoric of Reaction: Perversity, Futility, Jeopardy*. Cambridge: Belknap P, 1991.

Holmes, Richard. *Dr. Johnson and Mr. Savage*. London: Hodder and Stoughton, 1993.

Horkheimer, Max, and Theodor Adorno. "The Culture Industry." In *Dialectic of Enlightenment*. Trans. John Cumming. New York: Herder and Herder, 1972. 120–67.

Hudson, Nicholas. *Samuel Johnson and Eighteenth-Century Thought*. Oxford: Clarendon P, 1988.

Hume, David. *A Treatise of Human Nature*. Ed. L. A. Selby-Bigge. 2d ed. Oxford: Oxford UP, 1978.

Ignatieff, Michael. *The Needs of Strangers*. New York: Viking Penguin, 1985.

Jack, Ian. *Augustan Satire: Intention and Idiom in English Poetry, 1660–1750*. Oxford: Clarendon P, 1957.

Johnson, Samuel. *An Account of the Life of Mr. Richard Savage*. Ed. Clarence Tracy. Oxford: Clarendon P, 1971.

——. *The Adventurer and The Idler*. Vol. 2 of *The Yale Edition of the Works of Samuel Johnson*. Ed. W. J. Bate, J. M. Bullitt, and L. F. Powell. New Haven: Yale UP, 1963.

——. *Diaries, Prayers, and Annals.* Vol. 1 of *The Yale Edition of the Works of Samuel Johnson.* Ed. E. L. McAdam Jr. and Donald and Mary Hyde. New Haven: Yale UP, 1958.

——. *The History of Rasselas, Prince of Abyssinia.* In *Rasselas and Other Tales.* Vol. 14 of *The Yale Edition of the Works of Samuel Johnson.* Ed. Gwin Kolb. New Haven: Yale UP, 1990.

——. *Lives of the English Poets.* 3 vols. Ed. G. B. Hill. Oxford: Clarendon P, 1905.

——. *Poems.* Vol. 6 of *The Yale Edition of the Works of Samuel Johnson.* Ed. E. L. McAdam and George Milne. New Haven: Yale UP, 1964.

——. *Political Writings.* Vol. 10 of *The Yale Edition of the Works of Samuel Johnson.* Ed. Donald Greene. New Haven: Yale UP, 1977.

——. "Preface to a Dictionary of the English Language." *Samuel Johnson: Rasselas, Poems, and Selected Prose.* Ed. Bertrand H. Bronson. 3d ed. New York: Holt, Rinehart, and Winston, 1971. 234–60.

——. "Preface to Shakespeare." *Johnson on Shakespeare.* Vol. 7 of *The Yale Edition of the Works of Samuel Johnson.* Ed. Arthur Sherbo. New Haven: Yale UP, 1968.

——. *The Rambler.* Vols. 3–5 of *The Yale Edition of the Works of Samuel Johnson.* Ed. W. J. Bate and Albrecht B. Strauss. New Haven: Yale UP, 1969.

Juvenal. "Satire X." *Juvenal and Persius.* Trans. G. G. Ramsay. Cambridge: Harvard UP, 1918. 192–220.

Kernan, Alvin. *Samuel Johnson and the Impact of Print.* Princeton: Princeton UP, 1987.

Krutch, Joseph Wood. *Samuel Johnson.* New York: Henry Holt, 1944.

Larsen, Lyle. *Dr. Johnson's Household.* Hamden, Conn.: Archon Books, 1985.

Lascelles, Mary. "Johnson and Juvenal." *New Light on Dr. Johnson.* Ed. F. W. Hilles. New Haven: Yale UP, 1959. 35–55.

Linebaugh, Peter. *The London Hanged: Crime and Civil Society in the Eighteenth Century.* Cambridge: Cambridge UP, 1992.

Lipking, Lawrence. *The Ordering of the Arts in Eighteenth-Century England.* Princeton: Princeton UP, 1970.

Lukács, Georg. *Studies in European Realism.* New York: Grosset and Dunlap, 1964.

Lynch, Deidre. "'Beating the Track of the Alphabet': Samuel Johnson, Tourism, and the ABCs of Modern Authority." *ELH* 57 (1990): 357–405.

Lynn, Steven. *Samuel Johnson after Deconstruction.* Carbondale: Southern Illinois UP, 1992.

Lyotard, Jean-François. *Just Gaming*. Trans. Wlad Godzich. Minneapolis: U of Minnesota P, 1985.

Mandeville, Bernard. *The Fable of the Bees*. Harmondsworth: Penguin Books, 1989.

Maner, Martin. "Satire and Sympathy in Johnson's *Life of Savage*." *Genre* 8 (1975): 107–18.

Marshall, Dorothy. *Dr. Johnson's London*. New York: John Wiley and Sons, 1968.

Miner, Earl. "Dr. Johnson, Mandeville, and 'Publick Benefit.'" *HLQ* 21 (1958): 159–66.

Mullan, John. *Sentiment and Sensibility*. Oxford: Oxford UP, 1988.

O'Flaherty, Patrick. "Johnson as Satirist: A New Look at *The Vanity of Human Wishes*." *ELH* 34 (1967): 78–91.

O'Shaughnessy, Toni. "Fiction as Truth: Personal Identity in Johnson's *Life of Savage*." *Studies in English Literature* 30 (1990): 487–501.

Patey, Douglas Lane. *Probability and Literary Form: Philosophic Theory and Literary Practice in the Augustan Age*. Cambridge: Cambridge UP, 1984.

Piozzi, Hester. *Anecdotes of the Late Samuel Johnson*. Vol. 1 of *Johnsonian Miscellanies*. Ed. G. B. Hill. New York: Barnes and Noble, 1966.

Pocock, J. G. A. *The Machiavellian Moment: Florentine Political Thought and the Atlantic Republican Tradition*. Princeton: Princeton UP, 1975.

———. *Virtue, Commerce, and History: Essays on Political Thought and History, Chiefly in the Eighteenth Century*. Cambridge: Cambridge UP, 1985.

Porter, Roy. *English Society in the Eighteenth Century*. Harmondsworth: Penguin Books, 1990.

Richardson, Samuel. *Clarissa*. 4 vols. New York: Dent and Dutton, 1967.

Rudé, George. *The Crowd in History, 1730–1848*. New York: John Wiley and Sons, 1964.

———. *Hanoverian London: 1714–1808*. Berkeley and Los Angeles: U of California P, 1971.

———. *Wilkes and Liberty*. Oxford: Clarendon P, 1962.

Sachs, Arieh. *Passionate Intelligence: Imagination and Reason in the Work of Samuel Johnson*. Baltimore: Johns Hopkins UP, 1967.

Schwartz, Richard B. *Daily Life in Johnson's London*. Madison: U of Wisconsin P, 1983.

Selby-Bigge, L. A. "Introduction." *British Moralists, Being Selections from Writers Principally of the Eighteenth Century*. Ed. L. A. Selby-Bigge. Indianapolis: Bobbs-Merrill, 1964.

Sennett, Richard. *The Fall of Public Man: On the Social Psychology of Capitalism*. New York: Vintage, 1978.

Shaftesbury, Anthony, Earl of. *Characteristic of Men, Manners, Opinion, Times, Etc.* Ed. John M. Robertson. London: Grant Richards, 1900.

Smith, Adam. *An Inquiry into the Nature and Causes of the Wealth of Nations.* Ed. Edwin Cannan. Chicago: U of Chicago P, 1976.

Stallybrass, Peter, and Allon White. *The Politics and Poetics of Transgression.* Ithaca: Cornell UP, 1986.

Stauffer, Donald. *The Art of Biography in Eighteenth-Century England.* Princeton: Princeton UP, 1941.

Thompson, E. P. "The Moral Economy of the English Crowd in the Eighteenth Century." In *Customs in Common.* New York: The New Press, 1991. 185–258.

Tomarken, Edward. *Johnson, Rasselas, and the Choice of Criticism.* Lexington: University Press of Kentucky, 1989.

Tracy, Clarence. *The Artificial Bastard: A Biography of Richard Savage.* Cambridge: Cambridge UP, 1953.

Trowbridge, Hoyt. "Scattered Atoms of Probability." *Eighteenth-Century Studies* 5:1 (1971): 1–38.

Vesterman, William. "Johnson and *The Life of Savage.*" *ELH* 36 (1969): 659–78.

———. *The Stylistic Life of Samuel Johnson.* New Brunswick: Rutgers UP, 1977.

Voitle, Robert. *Samuel Johnson the Moralist.* Cambridge: Harvard UP, 1961.

Wain, John. *Samuel Johnson.* New York: Viking, 1974.

Watt, Ian. "Publishers and Sinners: The Augustan View." Vol. 12 of *Studies in Bibliography.* Ed. Fredson Bowers; Bibliographical Society of Virginia. Charlottesville: U of Virginia P, 1959. 3–20.

———. *The Rise of the Novel.* Berkeley and Los Angeles: U of California P, 1957.

Weinbrot, Howard. *The Formal Strain.* Chicago: U of Chicago P, 1969.

Wharton, T. F. *Samuel Johnson and the Theme of Hope.* London: Macmillan, 1984.

Wimsatt, William K. "The Concrete Universal." In *The Verbal Icon: Studies in the Meaning of Poetry.* Lexington: University Press of Kentucky, 1954. 69–83.

———. *Philosophic Words: A Study of Style and Meaning in "The Rambler" and "Dictionary" of Samuel Johnson.* New Haven: Yale UP, 1948.

———. "The Structure of Romantic Nature Imagery." In *The Verbal Icon: Studies in the Meaning of Poetry.* Lexington: University Press of Kentucky, 1954. 103–16.

Wordsworth, William. *The Prelude 1799, 1805, 1850.* Ed. Jonathan Wordsworth, M. H. Abrams, and Stephen Gill. New York: W. W. Norton, 1979.

Index

About the Author

Thomas Reinert is Visiting Assistant Professor of English at
Brandeis University.

Library of Congress Cataloging-in-Publication Data
Reinert, Thomas.
Regulating confusion : Samuel Johnson and the crowd / Thomas Reinert.
   p.   cm.
Includes bibliographical references and index.
ISBN 0-8223-1707-9 (cloth : alk. paper). — ISBN 0-8223-1717-6 (pbk. : alk. paper)
1. Johnson, Samuel, 1709–1784—Political and social views.   2. Johnson, Samuel,
1709–1784. Dictionary of the English language.   3. Johnson, Samuel, 1709–
1784—Knowledge—Language and languages.   4. Literature and society—
England—History—18th century.   5. Social ethics—History—18th century.
6. Johnson, Samuel, 1709–1784—Ethics.   7. Collective behavior in
literature.   8. Social ethics in literature.   9. Crowds in literature.   I. Title.
PS3537.P6R44   1996
828'.609—dc20   95-32412